Dwayne's Guitar Lessons Presents:

Learn Guitar Chord Theory

By

Dwayne Jenkins

Published by Tritone Publishing

Introduction

When you learn to play the guitar, you will mainly be playing guitar chords. In some instances you will play melody. What is great about the guitar is that you can specialize in chords, melody, or both.

You can choose to just play chords (this is a specialty of rhythm players) and master harmony. Or you can be a lead guitar player (a specialty of playing solos) and master melody. I highly recommend you work at both.

In this book Learn Guitar Chord Theory we are going to just focus on guitar chords. How they are constructed and why they are called what they are. Major, minor, sus4, etc. This will give you a well rounded way of understanding guitar chords.

When it comes to guitar chords, there are literally thousands that can be created on the guitar. I know, crazy huh? How could you get so much from six strings and twelve frets? But it's true.

Although there are so many, we won't be learning them all. If that was the case, this book would never end. We're just going to get down the basics of how they are constructed and why they are called what they are.

Within the book I will be presenting you with examples and exercises that you will need to complete. This will allow you to judge your progress and make sure you fully understand the material.

Often when playing the guitar you are accompanying another musician like in a duet, or musicians like playing in a band. In doing so, you want to make sure you fully understand your role in the situation. This is where knowledge of chords comes in.

The role of the guitar player can be either lead, or rhythm. Both are just equally important, and should be learned. The purpose of this book will be to focus on guitar chords. These will give a better understanding in the direction of rhythm playing.

This will also help you in songwriting if you choose to do so in the future. The foundation of any contemporary song is the chords and chord progression. So if you're ready, let's take a look at how to create guitar chords.

Dwayne Jenkins

Table of Contents

Chapter 1 Chord Foundation

Lesson 1: The major triad

Music has been called many times over a science of mathematics. This makes sense considering that it deals with numbers (math) and formulas (science) when you learn to work with it. This is the case with guitar chords.

Guitar chords are the building blocks of music. They are notes taken out of the key they come from and they are built from there. Triads set up the foundation for all other chords to be built upon. A triad is a chord consisting of three notes.

Now before we can get into understanding guitar chords or chords in general, we must learn about the musical alphabet. Or otherwise known as the chromatic scale. These are the twelve notes that make up all of western music. These twelve notes are where all chords and scales come from.

The musical alphabet is made up of the letters A-G. With some accidentals (sharps/flats) in between the notes except for two. The notes are as follows: A A# B C C# D D# E F F# G G#. Can you see the two notes that don't have a sharp after them?

I say sharp/flat because they are the same notes, it just depends on which way you are moving along the scale. For instance, if you go up it is sharp. If you go down it is flat. So an A sharp is the same thing as a B flat, (A#/Bb) same note.

For our training purposes here, I will refer to notes either being sharpened (moved up a fret) or flattened (moving back) when it comes to creating different chords. To set the foundation, we will start with the Major triad.

The major triad consists of the 1, 3, & 5th note of any major scale that it is taken out of. To keep things simple, we will start with the key of C major. Why? Because it has no sharps or flat notes in it.

These sharps and flats are called "accidentals" in music terms. But to keep things simple they'll just be referred to as sharps or flats. If we look at the 12 note musical alphabet as roots of the music tree, then the major scale (Do Re Mi etc) will represent the tree trunk.

Then all the chords and scales that come out of the tree trunk will be the tree branches.

Musical alphabet = 12 music tree roots
Major scale (Do Re Mi) = music tree trunk (8 notes of the 12)
All chords and scales (major, minor, etc) = music tree branches.

As you can see, this analysis is fairly simple and easy to understand. And if you can wrap your head around the concept, it will make learning this material a lot easier.

So, back to the major triad. All major triads will be made up of this scientific formula. In the C major scale, we have the notes C D E F G A B C. If we give each note a number value, we can see it has 8 notes.

C	D	E	F	G	A	B	C
1	2	3	4	5	6	7	8
Do	Re	Mi	Fa	So	La	Ti	Do

To make our C major triad we use the 1 3 5. In this case it will be the C, E, & G. This will be the same for all major chords. The notes will be different, but the chord formula will be the same. Let's look at another key. The key of G major.

G major consists of G A B C D E F# G. In this scale the F is sharpened to fit into the Do Re Mi I mentioned earlier. All major scales must have this. If a scale does not have this sound, it is not a major scale.

If you can hear the Do Re Mi when playing your guitar, you will be able to find all 8 notes in any major scale. In the case of G major, you will see that if you use the natural F note, it won't sound correct.

In order for it to sound correct, it must be sharpened. To create the G major triad we use the same formula. The 1 3 5. These notes will be the G B & D. Same formula, just different notes. This will be for all twelve keys in the music alphabet.

Now to view these so we can easily play them on the guitar, we want to learn how to read chord charts. These are diagrams that show where the note locations are.

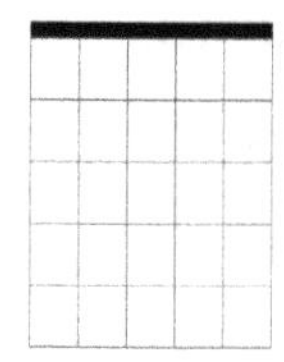

The vertical lines represent the six guitar strings from biggest on the left and smallest on the right. The horizontal lines represent the frets. The highlighted horizontal line represents the nut where the strings go through.

This will be our reference guide for creating guitar chords. Look at it like the guitar is facing upward.

Here are diagrams of the two major triads we have learned so far.

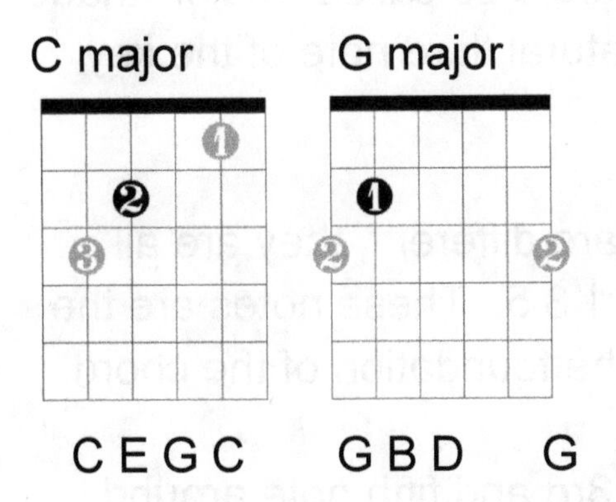

If you look at the chord diagrams, they tell us where to put our fingers to form these chords. It also lets us know where the notes of these major triads are located on the fretboard. This gives us a great reference guide for quickly finding these chords and forming them.

Since there are thousands of chords that can be formed, I won't go through all of them. Just the most common ones found in contemporary songs.

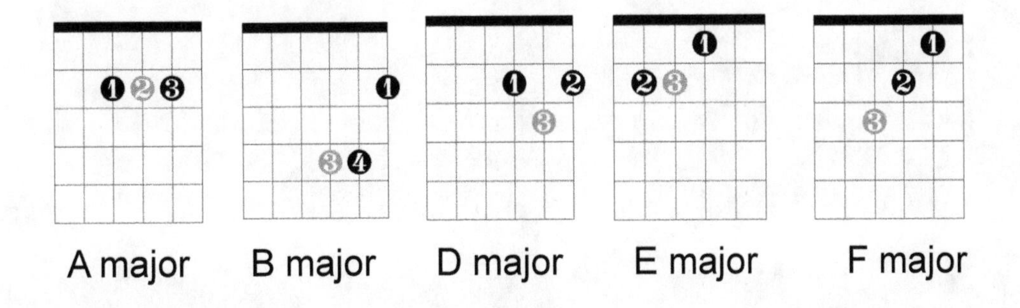

I left out the C and G because I presented them earlier. But as you can see, all these chords are made up of three notes. That is why they are called triads. They are also called “major” triads because they are made up of the natural third note of the key they are created out of.

Remember, even though the notes are different, they are all made up of the same formula. The 1 3 5. These notes are the most important because they form the foundation of the chord.

As you will see, when we move the 3rd and fifth note around (the 1 will stay the same as that is the root) it will allow us to create different chords.

Now see if you can find the Do Re Mi Fa So La Ti Do in the other keys and then find the 1 3 5 to create the major triad. You should be able to do this with all 12 notes in the musical alphabet.

Lesson 2: The minor triad

The minor triad is the same thing. A chord made up of three notes. Except with this chord (and all minor triads in any key) we flatten the third note by one fret. This allows us to create a bit of a "sad" sound out of this chord.

As we continue down the road of chord construction, we are going to clearly see how the sound of different chords allow us to create different emotions. Majors and minor chords will have different characteristics.

If we look at the C major triad (C E G) and we flatten the third note by one fret, we now have C Eb & G. This will be the same for all minor triads. Now we can do this with all of the major triads that we have learned so far.

The G major triad G B D can now be converted to a minor triad by flattening the third note. We now have G Bb and D. See how easy this is in theory? Now we just need to find these notes in our chord shapes to make the conversion.

The first two triads we learned were the C major, and G major. We have now flattened the third note in each chord to make them a minor triad.

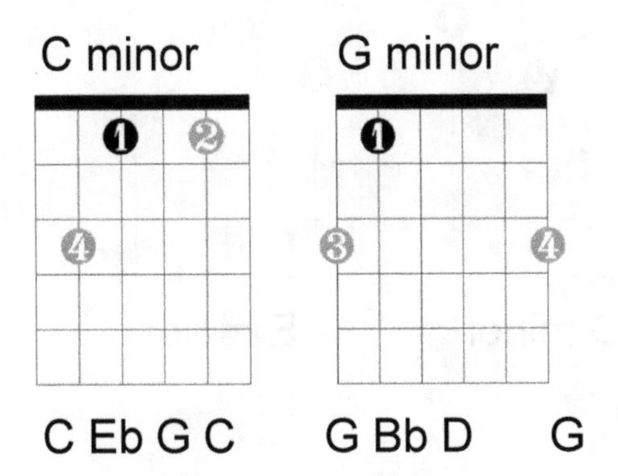

As you can see from the diagram above, we have moved one note back by one fret. In these two chords, that would be the third note. The notes are different, but the formula is the same. The 1 b3 5. Both of these chords also use open notes for the fifth. Notes that are not fretted.

Although, this is not always the case. In some instances, because of note location in these open positions, some chords will not be able to be formed, and will have to be formed further up the neck.

This is where such things as barre chords come in. We will discuss those later in the training.

For now let's look at the other minor triads of the majors that we have learned so far.

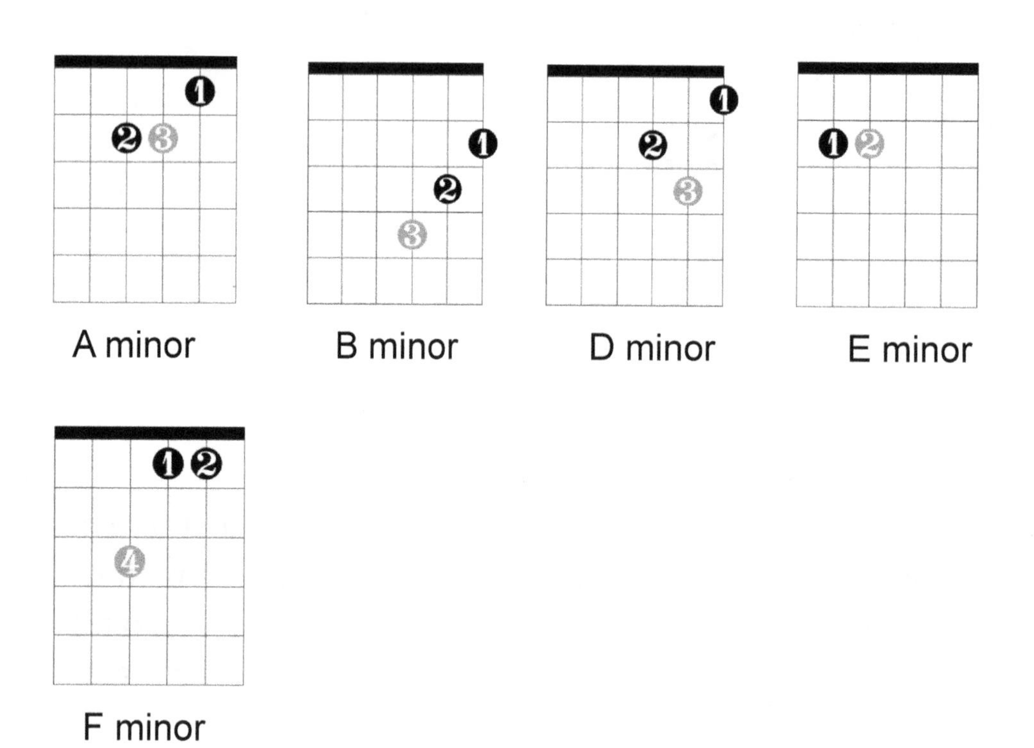

Here we have the other major triads converted to their minor counterparts. As you can see like with the C and G triads, we just moved one note back by one fret. In all these chords it is the third note that has been moved.

One thing to take note of is the E minor triad. Since the third note was already on the first fret and we can't go back past the nut, we just take our finger off the first fret and use the open D note.

Whenever we have a note on the first fret that needs to be flattened by one fret, we just take our finger off and use the open string note. Each string has a name for this reason. If you're not sure what the names of the six strings are, I'll show you here.

1=high**E** 2=**B** 3=**G** 4=**D** 5=**A** 6=low**E**

To remember your guitar strings, an easy way is to use an acronym. From the high E string to the low E string it could be, **E**aster **B**unnies **G**oes **D**ancing **A**fter **E**aster. Or from low to high could be **E**ddie **A**te **D**ynamite, **G**ood**B**ye **E**ddie.

It doesn't really matter how you do it, it just matters that you remember the string names as they will help in creating chords. It is also recommended that you learn the notes along the fretboard. This will make a huge difference.

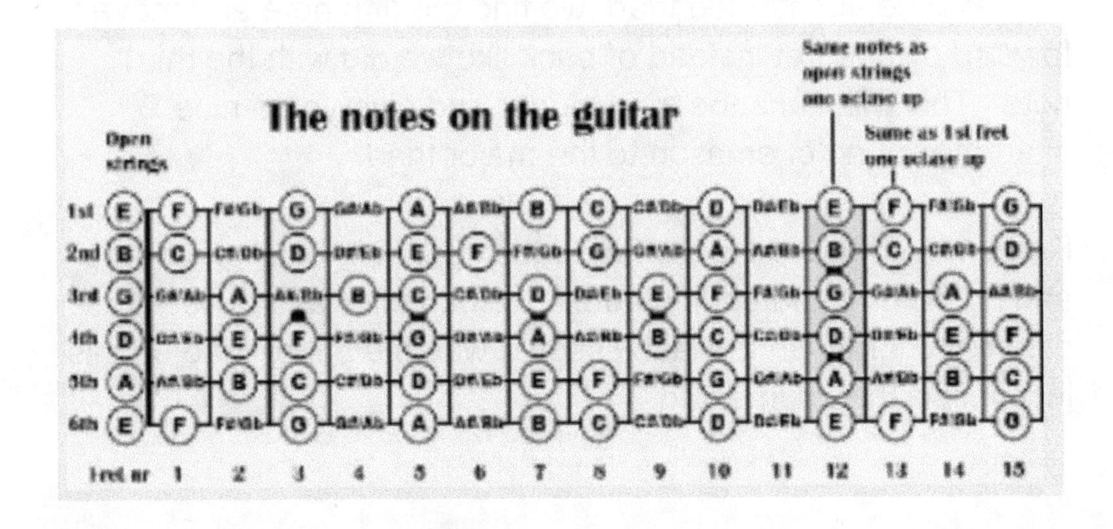

Lesson 3: The augmented triad

Augmented means to make it bigger. Like augmented breast surgery. To make them bigger. This can be done with our triads as well. This is done by sharpening the fifth note in the triad.

In the last lesson we learned that we can turn the major into a minor by flattening the third note. Now we look at how to make an augmented triad by sharpening the fifth note by one fret. This will give the triad another shade of color.

Can you see why it is a good idea to know your notes? By knowing your notes, knowing what notes are in the triad to begin with and where they're located, you will be able to find the note to move within the chord quickly and easily.

To make the augmented triad, we find the fifth note and move it forward by one fret instead of back like we did with the third note. This will make the triad bigger and give you a nice alternate sound of emotion to the major triad.

Remember, the triad is the foundation building block of chords and by moving and adding notes, we can alter and build different chords. In the last lesson it was the minor triad, in this lesson it is the augmented.

Like before, we'll take the C and G major triads and convert them into augmented triads.

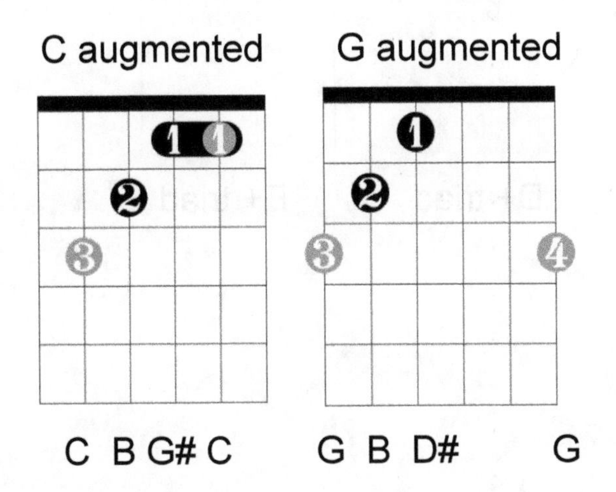

Here we can see that we sharpened the fifth note of the chord. Since both the C and G major use open notes for the fifth, we just sharpen that note by placing our finger on the first fret.

Most times in music, an augmented chord will have a (+) symbol. So instead of A augmented, it will be A +.

Let's look at converting the other major triads into augmented triads by sharpening the fifth note.

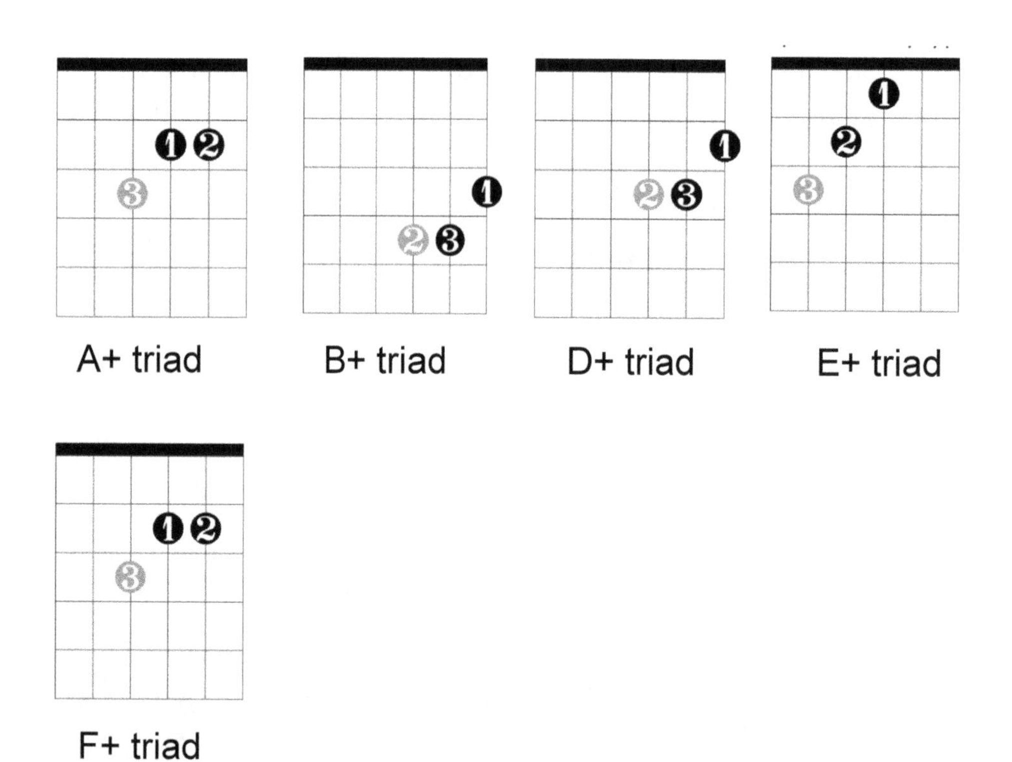

As we can see once again, we have three note chords and all we did was find the fifth note in the triad and move it up by one fret. Like we did with the minor triads, except instead of the third note back, we moved the fifth note forward.

Like I said before, in order for this to work you need to know what notes are in the chord and where they are located. This will allow you to make these chords quickly and easily. Doing this will allow you to get more out of the three note triad.

Also take note of the chord shapes. As you begin to switch notes around you'll see the shapes to be similar to others.

Like for instance, you can see that an E augmented triad looks the same as a C major triad. The B and D augmented triads are the same shape, just on different frets. And the A and F augmented triads are on the same fret.

So how could they be different chords?

Well, it's because of the location of the notes. To the untrained eye, this might seem incorrect, but to someone who knows their notes along the fretboard (hopefully that's you by now) you can clearly see why this is so.

This is what makes chord theory and music in general confusing. Because of the location of notes within the chords, they can actually be two different chords within the same shape.

Like the E augmented triad can also be a C major triad. It just depends on the root of the chord. This is the 1 of the chord. This is how you create thousands of chords in music.

As we learn more chord shapes, you will begin to see more and more of this. Don't worry. As long as you know your notes, you'll be fine.

Lesson 4: The diminished triad

These are where we make the chord smaller. Kind of like a double minor chord. I say this because we are now going to not only flatten the third note, but we are also going to flatten the fifth note.

We now know how to create a major triad, (1 3 5) the minor triad, (1 b3 5) the augmented triad, (1 3 #5) and now the diminished triad. This will be the 1 b3 b5. See how we flatten two notes this time?

The root of the chord (the 1) will always stay where it's at. Because if it moved, it would change into another chord. So we keep that one where it's at and move the other two notes around to create different shades of color.

After we get the most out of these three notes, we then move to adding additional notes to the foundational triad to create other chords. Like I said, this is how you can create thousands of chords. Knowing guitar chord theory.

Of course knowing it is one thing and applying it to the guitar is something else. So make sure to do that as you learn these different chords. Find them on your guitar and play them. Get used to how they sound.

Let's look at some diminished triads starting with the C triad again. Since we already know how to make a C minor triad, this shouldn't be too difficult. We just need to figure out which one of the other two notes is the fifth note and its location.

Now being that the fifth note in this and the G triad use open strings and we can't go past the nut, we will need to play these notes elsewhere. Like on a different string. Or possibly, move the whole triad altogether.

C diminished

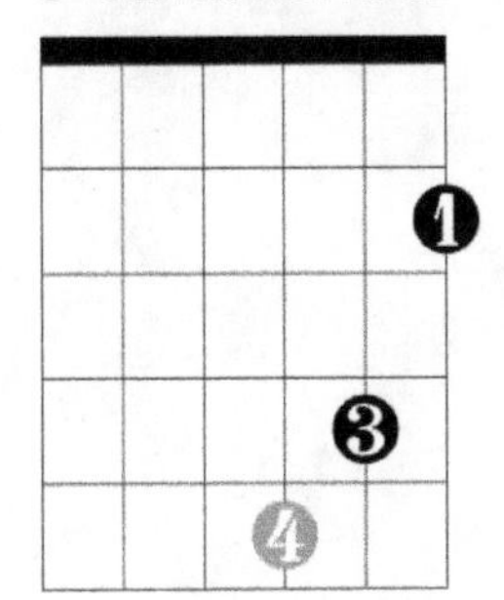

C D# F#

In the case of the C diminished triad, we have moved the notes around. The flattened third would be fine at the first fret, but the fifth note is an open note. So we couldn't make the triad in its current position.

But if we move the notes around as seen in the chord chart, we can form it in a new position.

This is the benefit of knowing not only the notes in the chord, but also where these notes are located on the fretboard. If you study the fretboard well enough, you'll see these notes all over the place. You could form this chord in multiple places.

Same goes for the G diminished triad. The flat third would be fine at the first fret, but the fifth note is open and we can't go past the nut. So we need to make some alterations.

G diminished

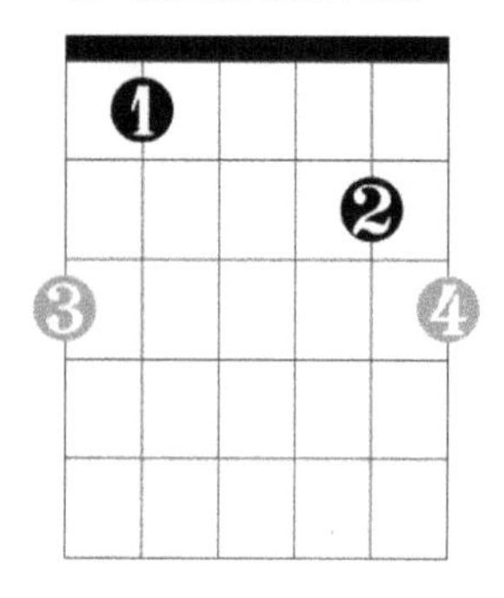

G Bb Db G

In this example, I kept the notes in the same location as the minor triad, the only difference is that I put the Db note on the second string. Like I said before, there are many different places you can play this chord.

Now let's see how we can create diminished triads with the other chords we've learned in previous lessons. Remember, you flatten the third and fifth notes.

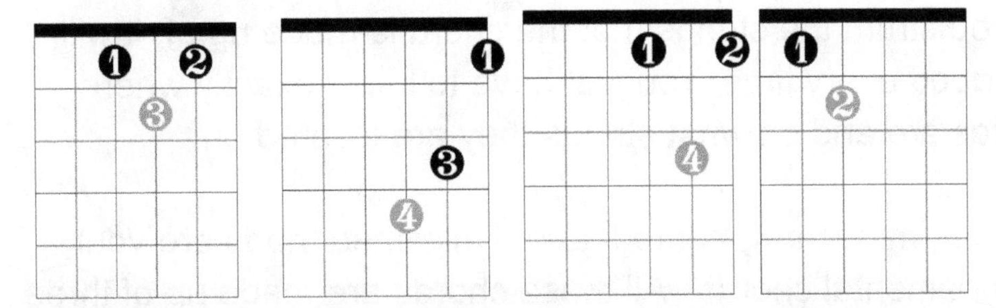

A diminished B diminished D diminished E diminished

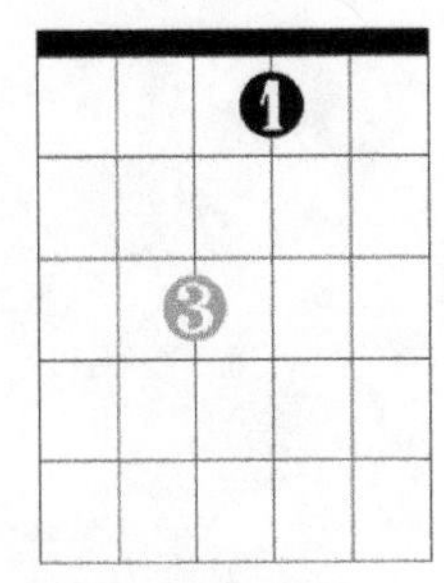

F diminished

If you go back and look at your minor triads, you'll see that all we did here was move the fifth note back. In some cases we just lifted off a finger to move the note back to the open position. Pretty simple huh?

When playing three note chords such as these, you want to focus on the strings they are made up of when you strum. Take note of this. Because sometimes, the open strings don't always fit within the chord, and will sound off when played.

But if you strum the strings that the chord is made up of, it will sound good every time. You just have to know exactly where the notes are and on what strings they are located on.

The major, minor, augmented, and diminished triads are your four fundamental chords. All these chords are made up of three notes and they provide the foundation for all other chord types to come.

The major triad 1 3 5
The minor triad 1 b3 5
The augmented triad 1 3 #5
The diminished triad 1 b3 b5

Make sure you know these chords very well before moving on. They will make understanding the other chords that much easier.

Lesson 5: Triad exercises

Now we come to the fun part. Where we see how well we've learned our lessons. Triad exercises. Like I mentioned before, music is a language. And like all other languages learned, we want to make sure we can read and write it.

So in this lesson I'll present you with some chord chart diagrams and I want you to fill them in with the proper note location. We'll go over what chords we have learned so far. Major, minor, augmented and diminished.

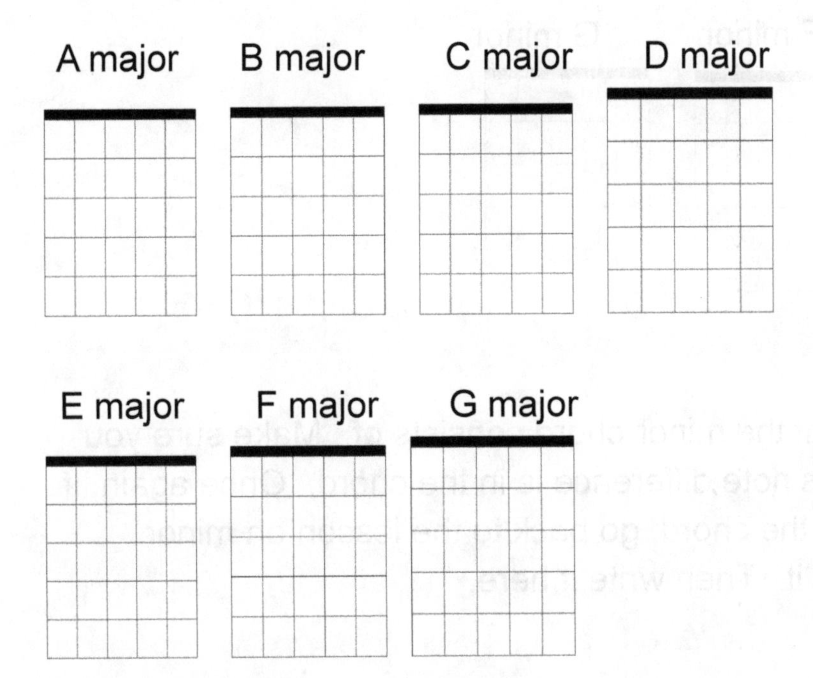

Go through and fill out these chord charts.

If you're not too sure where the notes are located, go back to the lesson and get the answer from there. It's ok to look at your notes. This is just a way to make sure you know these chords when you see them on paper.

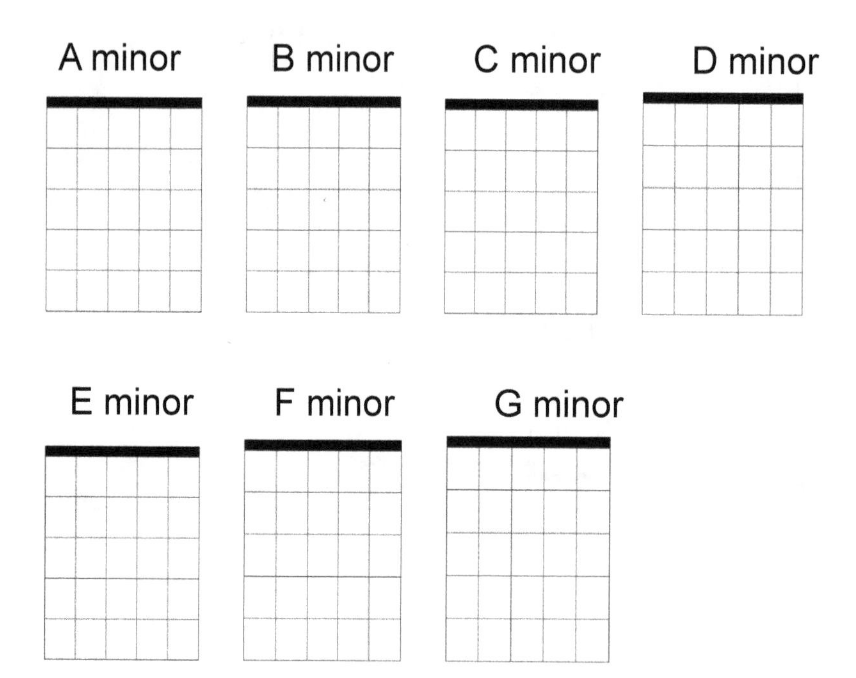

Remember what the minor chord consists of. Make sure you know where this note difference is in the chord. Once again, if you don't know the chord, go back to the lesson on minor chords and find it. Then write it here.

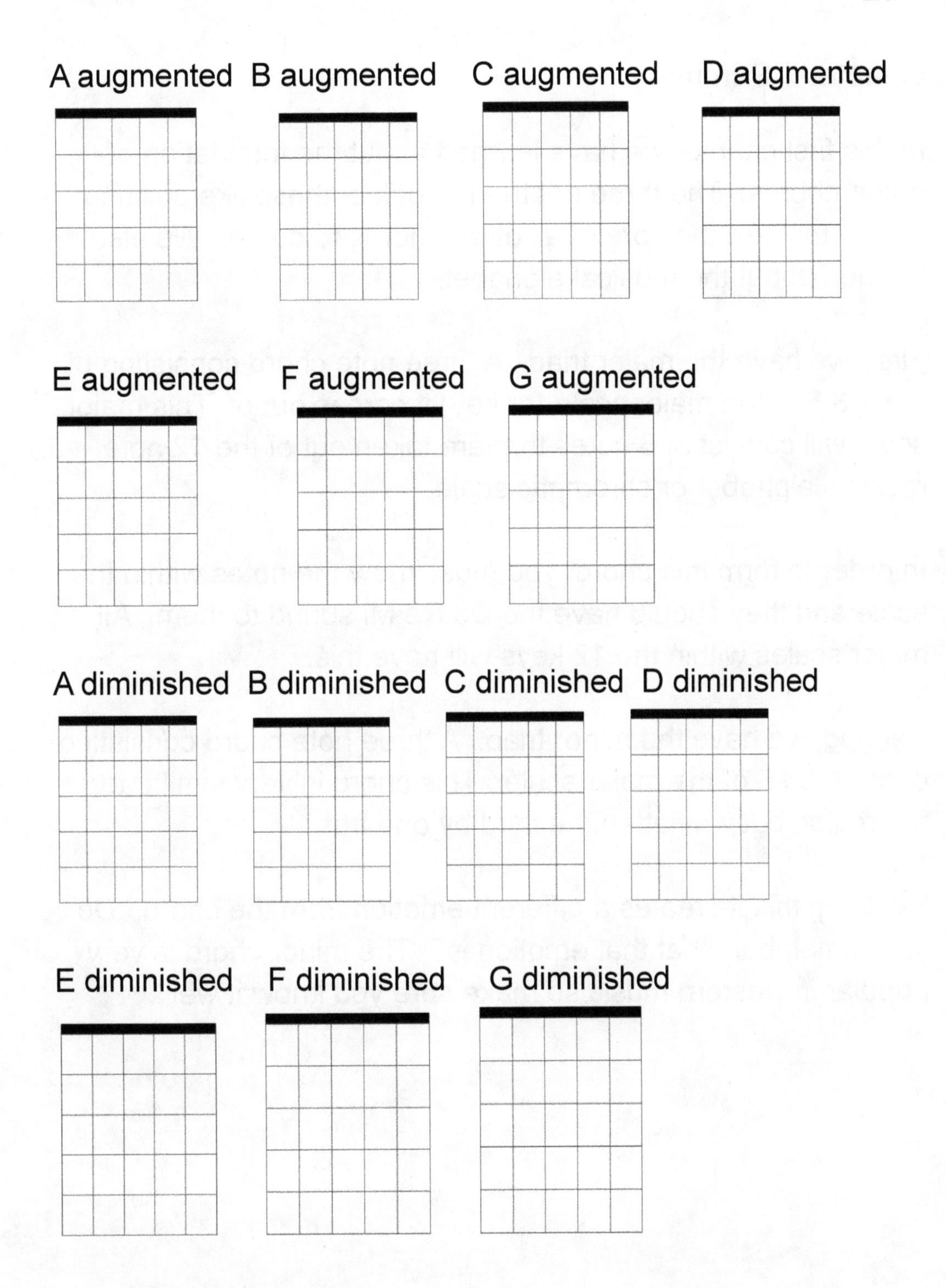
A augmented
B augmented
C augmented
D augmented
E augmented
F augmented
G augmented
A diminished
B diminished
C diminished
D diminished
E diminished
F diminished
G diminished

Chapter 1 Summary

In this first chapter we have learned about the foundation of guitar chords. The three not triad. Look at these like building blocks that are the core of all other chords to come. We also learned about the musical alphabet.

First, we have the major triad. A three note chord consisting of the 1 3 5 of the major scale (or key) it comes out of. This major scale will consist of 8 notes that are taken out of the 12 note musical alphabet or chromatic scale.

In order to form this chord, you must know the notes within the scale and they should have the Do Re Mi sound to them. All major scales within the 12 keys will have this.

Second, we have the minor triad. A three note chord consisting of the 1 b3 5 of the major scale. This chord is very similar to the major, but we flatten the third by one fret.

By doing this it creates a different emotion from the chord. Do you remember what that emotion is? The minor chord is very popular in western music so make sure you know it well.

Third, there is the augmented triad. This is where we make the chord bigger. We do this by sharpening (move forward) the fifth note in the chord. This allows us to create a different type of emotion.

If the fifth in the triad is a natural note we make it sharp. If it is a flattened note (Bb for example) we sharpen it to become natural. Knowing where this note is located within the chord is very important for this purpose.

Fourth, we have the diminished triad. This is where we flatten both the third and fifth notes. This is quite easy being that we flatten the third note for the minor and we sharpened the fifth for the augmented.

This is almost like a double minor chord. All we have to do is take the minor triad (with the already flat third) and add the flat fifth to it. Then we have a diminished triad.

Fifth, I provide you with some triad exercises. These are designed to make sure you fully understand the chapter on these fundamental chords. The better grasp you have of the fundamentals, the better off you'll be.

Make sure you write out these chords in the diagrams. It will help you to read and write the language of music. This will improve your guitar playing as well as your musicianship.

Chapter 2 Suspended & Sixth chords

Lesson 6: Suspended triads

A suspended triad is when we take the third note and move it forward to make it a four. Now we have 1 4 5. Or we could move it back two frets and have a 1 2 5. These are called sus chords. Sus being short for suspended.

Suspended means that you are suspending a note. In this case it is the third note suspended to the fourth or second position. What this does is create a new type of triad or chord voicing.

Since we know how to create the major triad, all we need to do now is move the third note up a fret for the sus4, or back two frets for the sus2.

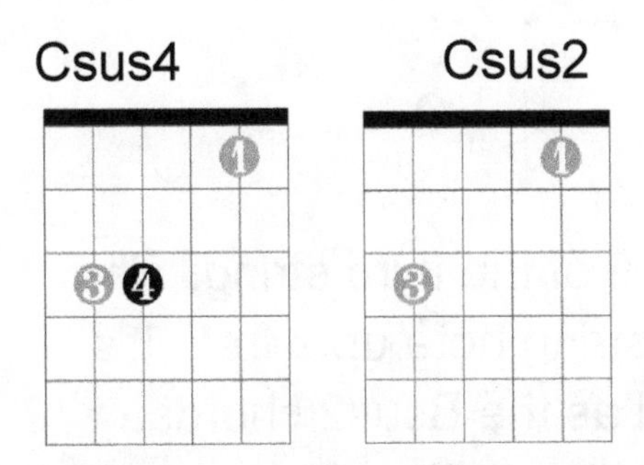

As we can see from the diagrams above, we have taken the third note of the C major triad (E) and moved it up a fret for the Csus4 chord, and back two frets for the Csus2 chord.

This allows us to have two more chord options. Now we have 6 different types of triads that we can make.

Major 1 3 5
Minor 1 b3 5
Augmented 1 3 #5
Diminished 1 b3 b5
Sus2 1 2 5
Sus4 1 4 5

Now we are really starting to build up a nice chord vocabulary. All by simply moving a few notes up and down the fretboard.

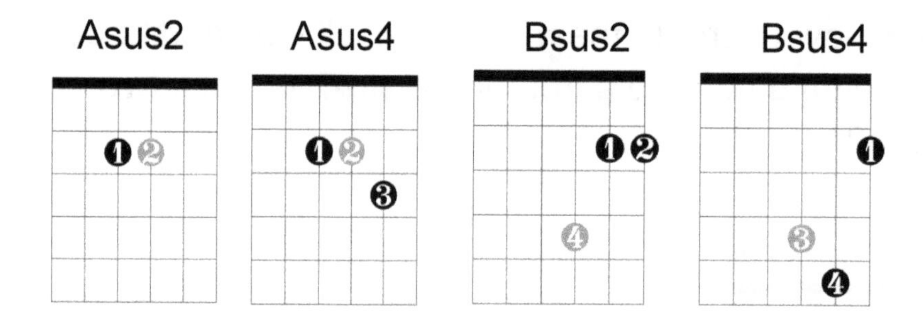

With the Asus2 we just take a finger off of the third string. The Asus4 chord we just moved the third string note up a fret. It's the same thing with the Bsus4 as well as the Bsus2 chords. You just move the 3rd to the 2nd and 4th position.

Let's look at a few more sus chords

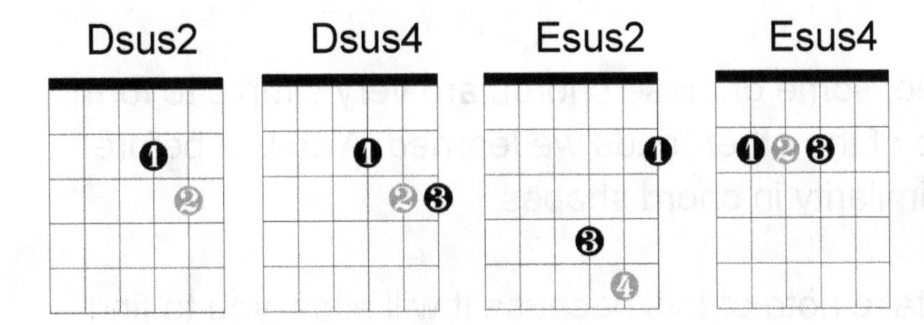

In the case of the Dsus2 chord, we just take our finger off of the first string, but move the note forward a fret for the Dsus4.

In the case of the Esus2, we move the whole chord to a different position for easier note location. But keep it in the main shape we've learned for the Esus4 chord.

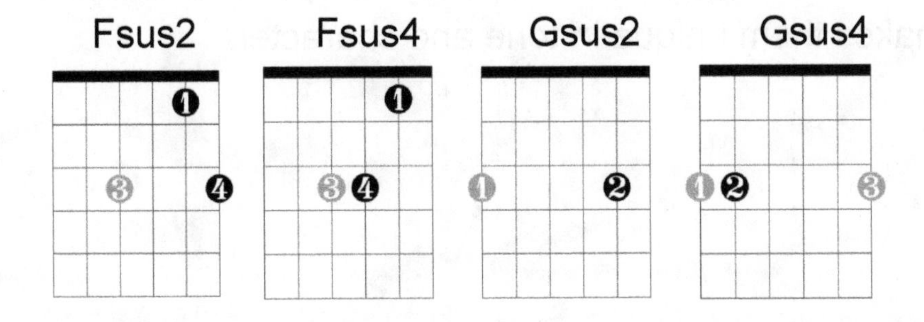

Same goes for these chords. The Fsus2 relocates the open note to the first string, but just moves it up a fret to make the Fsus4 chord. For the Gsus2 chord you just take your finger off of the A fifth string to play the open A note.

And for the Gsus4 chord, we just move the same note up a fret and place it under the root note on the 3rd fret.

As you can see, some of these chords are very simple to form. Just like some of the other triads we learned. Also like before, you'll notice similarity in chord shapes.

Make sure to take note of this because it will allow you to find chords quicker when they have the same shape.

If you think in patterns and shapes when it comes to learning to play the guitar, it will make learning the concepts and techniques associated with it a lot easier to learn.

Remember, suspended chords are not major or minor chords. They are kind of on their own because they "suspend" the third note. This makes them unique in tone and character.

Lesson 7: Major six chords

Now that we have learned about the foundation of guitar chords, we can now look at adding notes to it to make it bigger. This will give us even more emotion to work with. In addition to that, it will expand our knowledge of the fretboard.

What is also great about building the foundation with the triads that have been presented so far, is that it allows for easier understanding of chord formulas. With the major it's a 1 3 5, minor 1 b3 5, etc.

The major six chord just adds the 6th note in the scale to the major triad. So now we have a chord formula of 1 3 5 6.

Key of C major: C D E F G A B C
C major chord: 1 3 5= C E G
C major6 chord: 1 3 5 6= C E G A

See how simple this is? All we need to do now is just add the A note to the C major chord and we now have a C major6 chord. This is going to give us another shade of color to work with.

Let's start with the C and G chords like we did before.

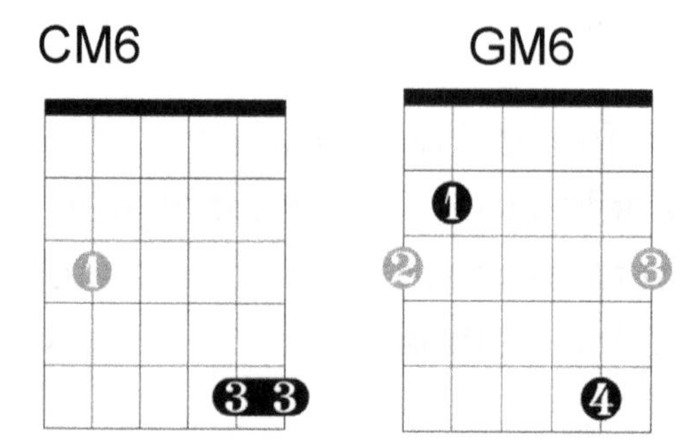

As we can see from the chord chart diagram, the notes have been moved around for the CM6 chord to make it easier to form. As where the GM6 chord has kept everything the same, just added a note on the second string 5th fret.

Sometimes these chords are just labeled as "6" chords and not necessarily "M6" chords. Same thing with major chords like G major. They'll sometimes just be labeled the name of the chord. Like G, A, B, etc. Not GMajor, or BMajor.

I'm telling you this so you don't get confused. One of the reasons music is hard to learn to read is because of the way it is written. Everyone writes it a bit different, and as you continue to study music, you'll see this to be true.

I'm writing it this way to keep it simple and allow for easier understanding of the concepts.

Major 6 chords

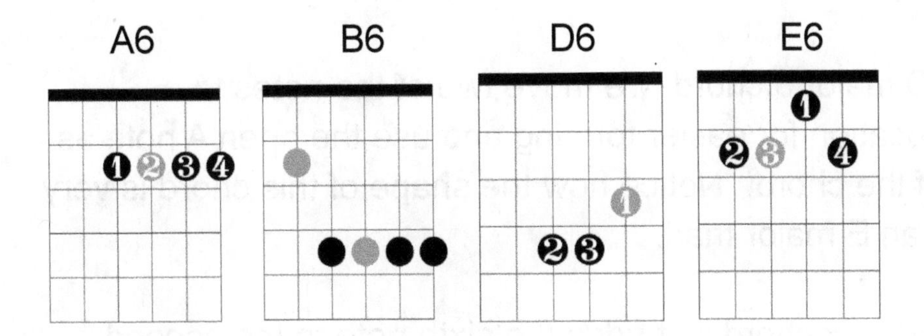

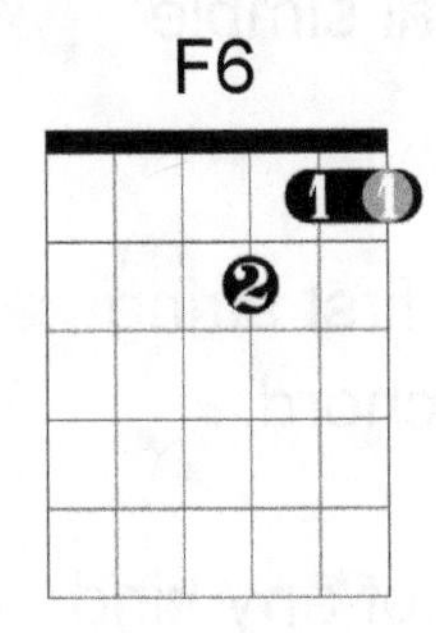

As we learned before with the other chords we learned, some notes will be moved to different locations to make them easier to form. And since we have these notes all over the fretboard, there is more than one way to form them.

The A major 6 chord is really simple to form, we just add another note to the triad on the first string 2nd fret.

Now the B major 6 chord is another story altogether. Here actually rearrange the shape to make this chord easier to form.

We can just barre all the notes on the 4th fret with our third finger and play the other one with our index finger.

With the D major 6 chord, we move two of the notes to a different location for easier forming and use the open A note as the fifth of the chord. Notice how the shape of this chord is very similar to an E major triad.

The E major six chord just adds the sixth note to the second string 2nd fret and keeps the triad where it's at. Real simple and easy to form.

And the F major 6 chord we move the F note to the first string 1st fret and use the open D string for the 6th in the chord.

What is most important when forming guitar chords of any kind is not necessarily the location of the notes (unless you're talking chord inversions, which we'll get to later in the training) but that the correct notes are in the chord.

In this case, the 1 3 5 6 will be in all the major 6 chords. No matter where these notes are located. You might have to move a note or two for easier forming, and if you know your notes well enough you can easily figure this out.

Look for other ways you can form the major 6 chord. There are many more examples, you just have to find them.

Lesson 8: Minor six chords

These chords are pretty easy to form as well now that we know the major sixth chords. All we need to do here is just flatten the third note and keep everything the same. The formula for the minor six chord will be 1 b3 5 6.

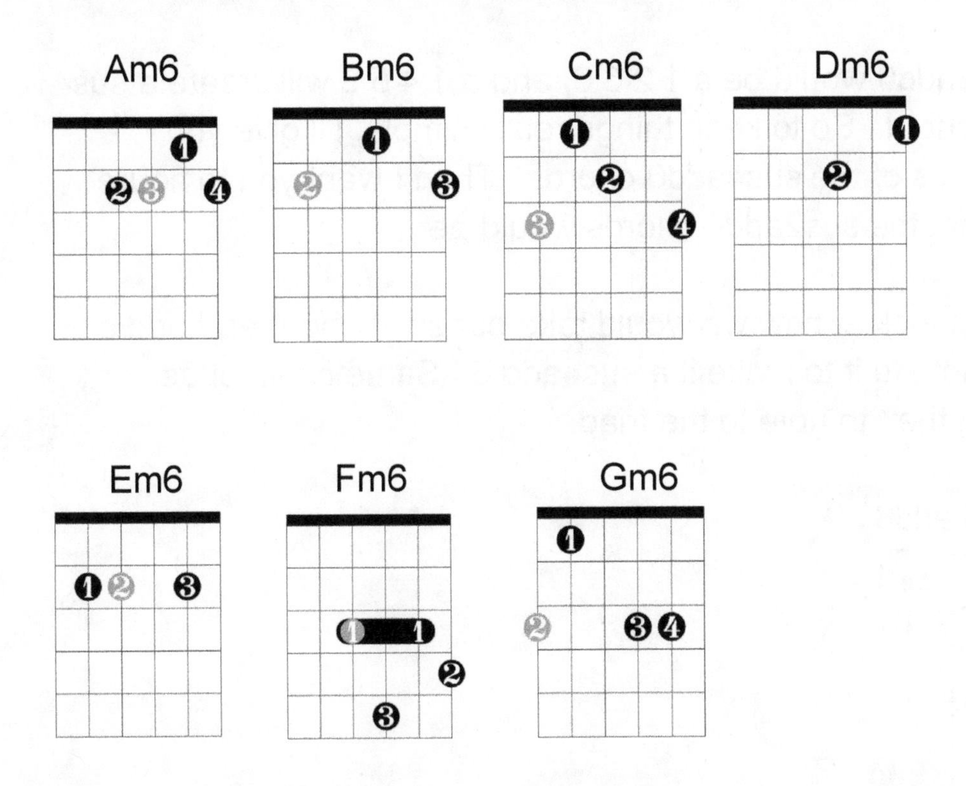

Since the notes in some of these chords are located in certain places, we need to change the location of the other notes to make the minor 6th chords. But as you can see, they all have the correct formula, 1 b3 5 6. See if you can find these chords elsewhere along the fretboard.

Lesson 9: Suspended add six chords

Now we can mix and match some options to create additional emotions with chords. When it comes to the suspended chords we have the sus2 and sus4. And since we've added the 6th note to the triad, we can create a suspended six chord.

A sus2add6 would be a 1 2 5 6, and a 1 4 5 6 will create a sus4 add6 chord. So to keep things really simple, I'll give you examples of the sus4add6 chords. Then I want you to figure out what the sus2add6 chords would be.

So let's look at how we would take our sus4 chord and add a sixth note to it to make it a sus4add 6. Same concept as adding the 6th note to the triad.

Csus4 add6

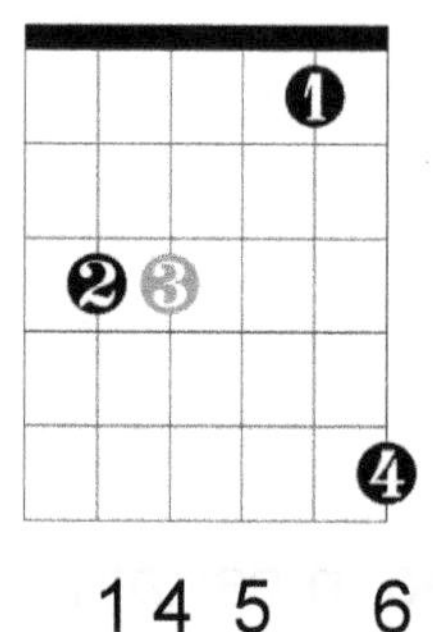

Can you see how we just took the Csus4 chord and added the sixth note to it? Now we have a new chord.

Let's look at how we can do this with the rest of the sus4 chords we've learned so far.

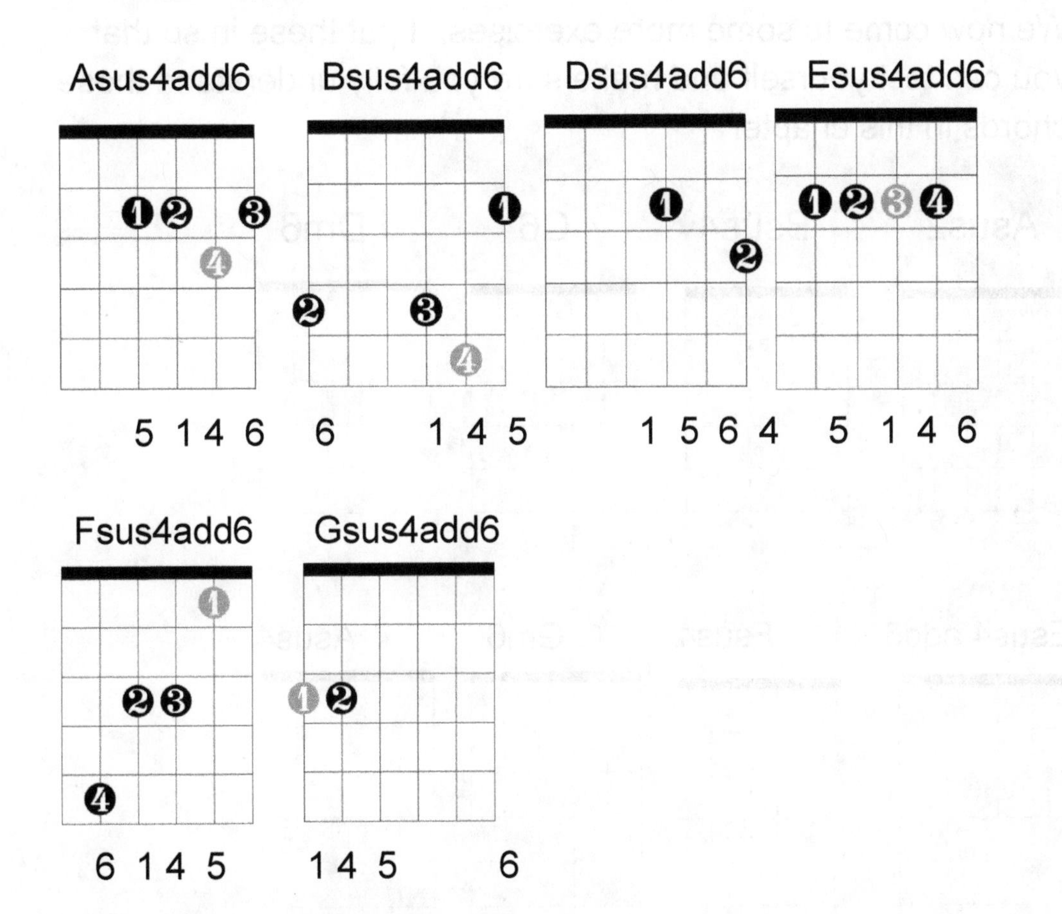

As we can see with all these chords, they have the sus4 formula with the added 6th note. We also notice that the notes aren't all in the same order. That's ok. They don't always need to have the 1 (root) as the lowest note.

Lesson 10: Sixth chord exercises

We now come to some more exercises. I put these in so that you can test yourself and make sure you fully understand these chords in this chapter

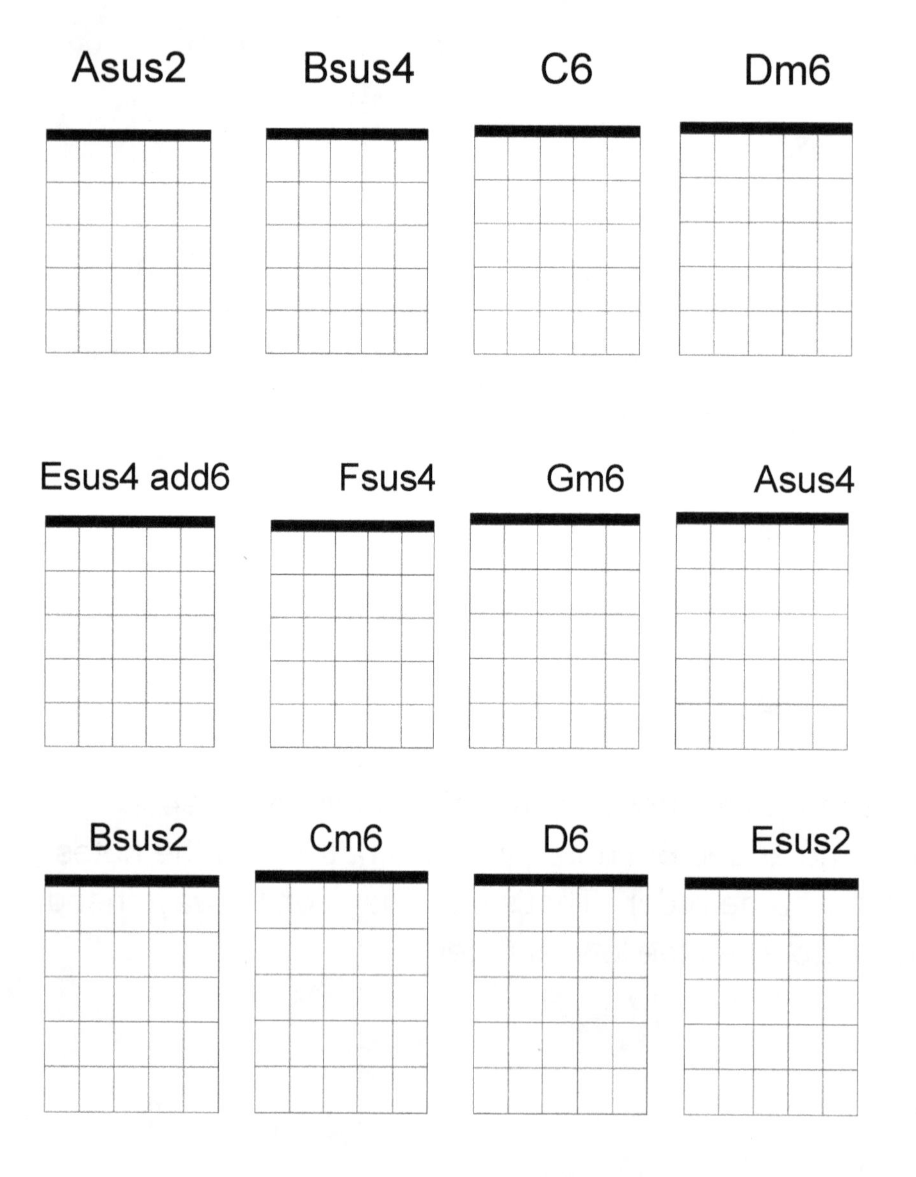

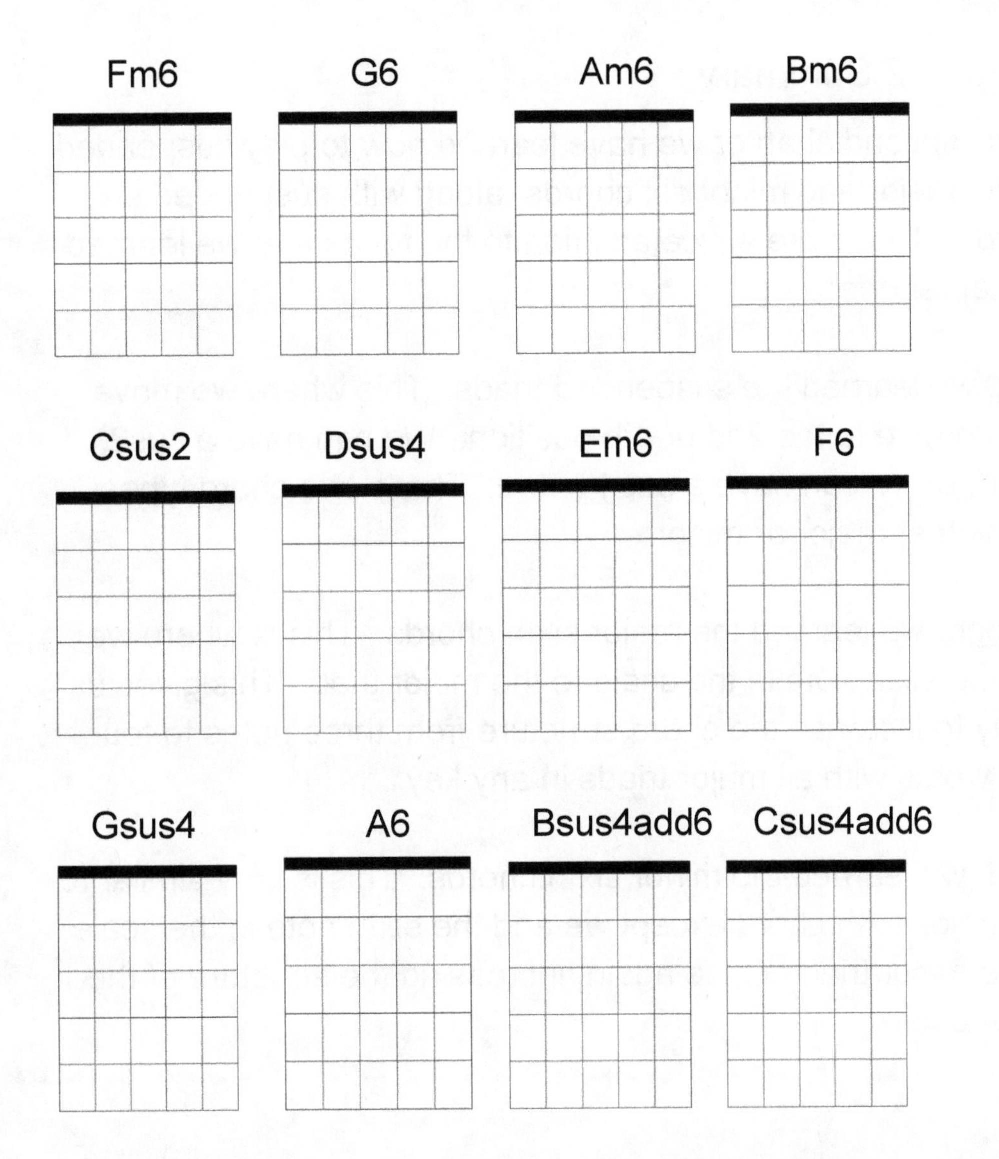

Go through these chords and make sure you firmly know how to read and write them. This will not only increase your chord vocabulary, but also increase your awareness of notes on the fretboard.

Chapter 2 Summary

In this second chapter we have learned how to play suspended triads, major and minor six chords, along with suspended six chords. These are a nice addition to the triads that we learned in chapter one.

First, we learned the suspended triads. This where we move the 3rd note to the 2nd or 4th position. We can have a sus2 chord, or we can have a sus4 chord. These two chord types are neither major or minor.

Second, we learned the major sixth chords. This is where we add the sixth note in the scale to the major triad. This gives us a way to increase the chord structure from three notes to four. This works with all major triads in any key.

Third, we learned the minor sixth chords. This is very similar to the major sixth chord except we add the sixth note in the scale to the minor triad. Once again, increasing the structure of the minor chord.

Fourth, we learned about how to mix the suspended chords and sixth chords together to create suspended six chords. This can also be known as an added sixth chord. Because we are adding the sixth note to the suspended triad.

Fifth, we go through exercises to make sure that we fully know how to form these chords. Remember, the suspended chord is made by "suspending" the third note back or forward. And the sixth chords are created by adding to the triads.

Study this chapter and make sure you know it well. For these chords help to build the foundation of guitar chord theory. And they will help with understanding future chords taught in this book. Along with others you'll learn in the future.

Once you learn these chords, work at trying to find them in other places on the fretboard. These can be played in multiple places. You just need to make sure you have the correct notes and know the chord formulas.

Make sure to study the chord formulas. Write them down and study them. The more you do this, the more it will become second nature. You will be able to create these chords at will for any occasion necessary.

Chapter 3 Seventh Chords

Lesson 11: Major seventh chords

Just like the major 6th chord, we look to the 7th note and add it to the triad. Now we have a chord formula of 1 3 5 7. Still a four note chord, but a little different sound.

Let's look at some major seventh chords.

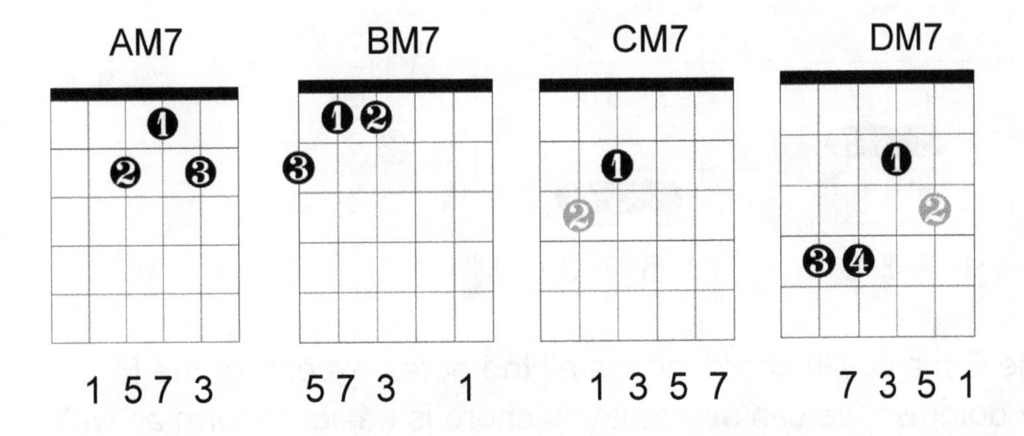

With the A major 7th chord we replace the A note on the third string with the open A note on the 5th string. This allows us to use the third string to add the 7th note to the chord shape.

With the B major 7th chord we have moved the notes entirely to a different position. This makes it easier to form. In this chord formation we use the open B note on the second string.

The C major 7th chord is even easier. We just take a finger off of the second string and have the 7th note open on the second string like the 5th note on the third string.

With the D major 7th we move the third note from the first string to the 4th string and we add the 7th note on the fifth string. By moving the third note, we can form this chord easier.

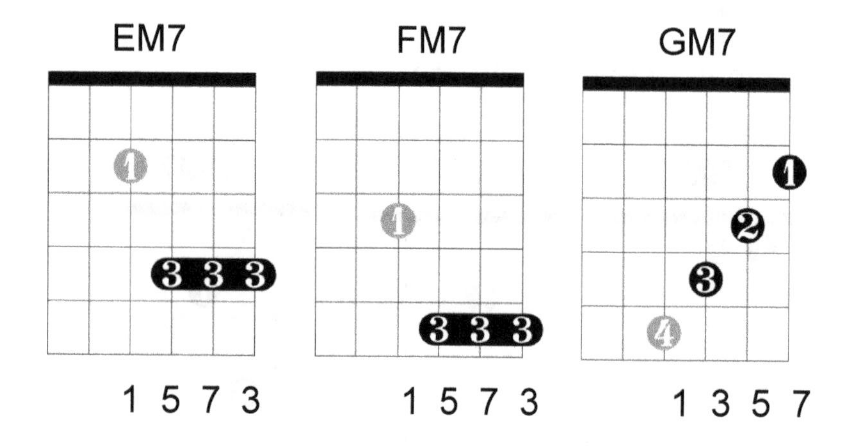

The E major 7th chord moves all the notes except for the E. By doing so we can see that this chord is easier to form as well. All other notes line up on the first three strings of the 4th fret.

The F major 7th chord is easy too as it is the same chord shape as the E, just one fret up. This makes it an easy transition between these two chords.

The G major 7th chord has also moved the notes. All of them. This makes it much easier to form as well.

As we can see from the chord charts, all the chords presented have the major 7th formula. 1 3 5 7. We don't have the 6th note, just the seventh. Same concept but a different note selection.

We can also see that the root note (the 1) isn't always the lowest note. And that's ok. This is just an inversion. As long as all the notes in the formula are presented, it's the correct chord.

We can also see that in some instances, we had to move the whole chord around to form it easier than just adding the 7th note to the common triad. You can see this with a few of the chords presented.

I chose these formations for easiest playability. This will give you a good place to start. Once you understand where the notes are at in the chords, you can then look at forming them elsewhere on the fretboard.

Look for ways that you can easily transition from one chord to another. Remember, forming them is step one and moving between them is step two.

Lesson 12: Minor seventh chords

These chords are similar except that we add the flat seventh note to the minor triad. This allows for even more of an alternate chord option. 1 b3 5 b7.

Let's look at some minor 7th chords:

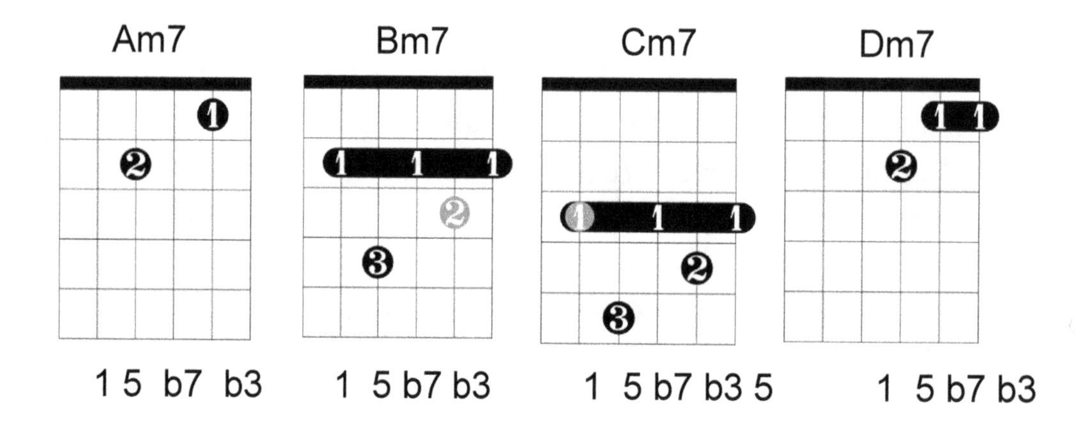

As we can clearly see, the chords all have the minor 7th formula with the flat 3rd and flat 7th notes. This flat seventh note makes these chords unique to the minor 6th chords that don't have a flat 6.

You can make a minor with a flat 6th note, but it would be a minor flat 6, and not a minor 6. The A minor 7th chord has just two fretted notes and the other two are open.

The B and C minor 7th chords use a barre across the 2nd and 3rd frets. Identical chords in different positions.

The D chord is really simple to form with a partial barre across two strings on the 1st fret.

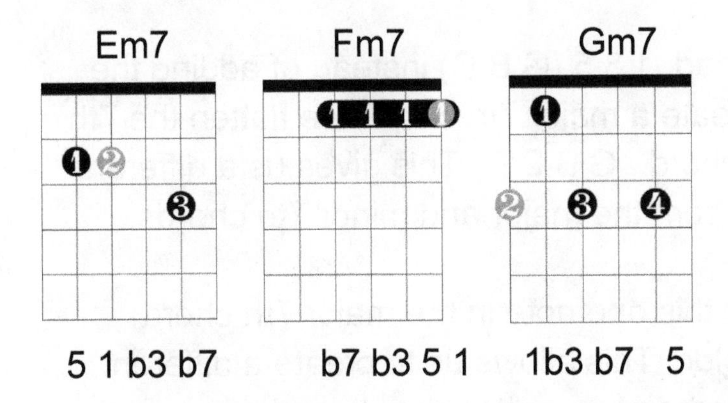

The E minor 7th chord just adds the note on the second string third fret.

The F minor 7th chord is easy to play as it is just a barre chord on the first four strings of the 1st fret.

And the G minor 7th chord is easy too. We just add the flat 7th note on the fourth string 3rd fret.

Remember, this is just one way of playing these chords. There are many, many different ways of playing them. Study notes on your fretboard and find other ways to form these chords.

Lesson 13: Dominant seventh chords

What's neat about the seventh chords is that we can flatten the 7th note and add a new chord. A dominant 7th chord. This is created by adding the flat 7 to the major triad.

Like in the G major triad, 1 3 5 (G B D) instead of adding the natural 7 (F#) and create a major 7th chord, we flatten the 7th note to create a G7 chord. G B D F. This gives us a different shade of color aside from the major and minor 7th chords.

Notice how flattening this one note in the major 7th chord creates a different color. This allows us to create a different shade of emotion. Remember, guitar chords and music in general is all about creating emotional content.

C major C7

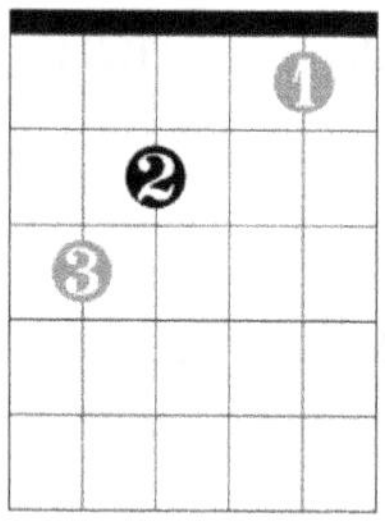

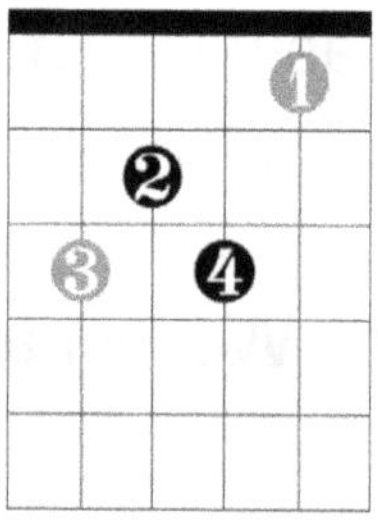

See how we just add the flat 7th note to the C major triad? Look at the C major 7th chord. You'll see it has the natural 7th note.

Now let's look at some more dominant 7th chords.

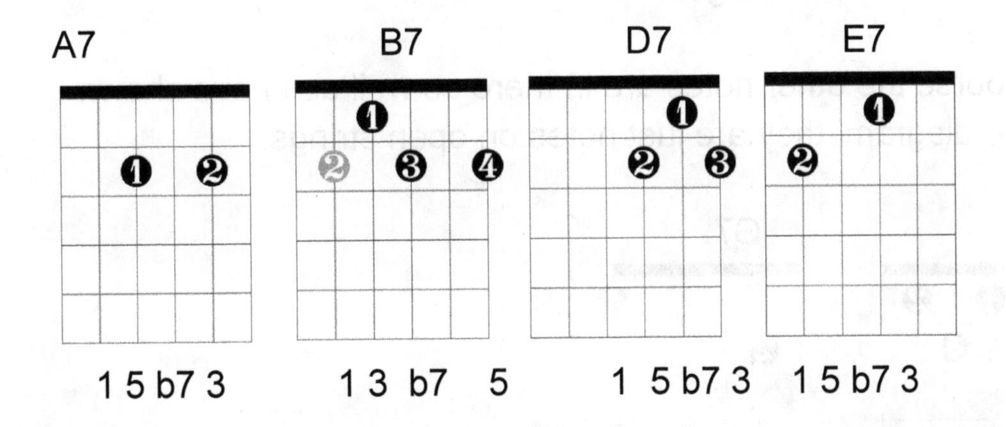

We can see that all these chords have the dominant seventh chord formula. 1 3 5 b7. We can also see that they are not too difficult to form.

Major 7: 1 3 5 7
Minor 7: 1 b3 5 b7
Dominant 7: 1 3 5 b7

The A7 chord is very easy to form with just two notes on the fourth and second strings 2nd fret.

The B7 chord is just a D7 chord shape on the fifth string with a note added to the first string 2nd fret.

The D7 chord is the same shape as the B7, just on the first three strings.

The E7 chord is even easier to form as it is only two notes on the fifth and third strings.

Of course the other notes are in there as well as I have shown in the diagram, they are just notes on open strings.

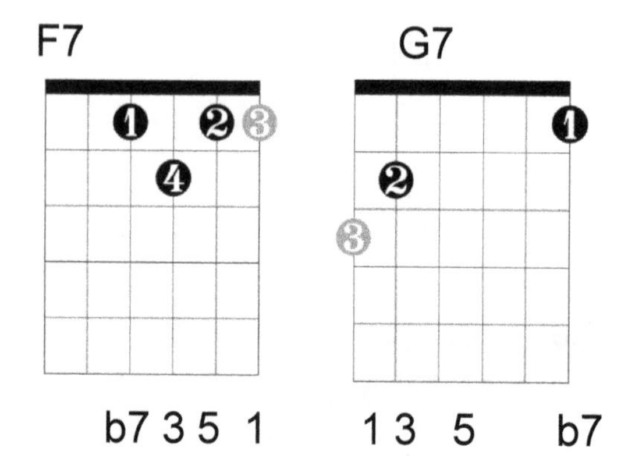

With the F7 chord we move the F note to the first string so we can put the b7 note on the fourth string 1st fret.

The G7 chord is really simple to create because all we need to do is move the note from the first string 3rd fret, to the 1st fret.

This change up in notes allows us to create a different type of sound that is very popular in guitar playing. These chords can be found in many different songs.

Remember, the natural 7th note is right next to the 8th note. So all you need to do is find it, and move it back by one fret.

Lesson 14: Suspended seventh chords

Just like the sixth chords, we can create suspended seventh chords. These will just have the b7th note in them instead of the natural. They will also be abbreviated to sus7 chords.

Once again, allowing us to mix and match chords to create new chords, or chord substitutes as they are sometimes called. These types of chords can be a bit confusing as they can have different names.

If we use the sus2 and add the b7 to the formula, it will be considered a 7sus2 chord. As in C7sus2. If we are using the 4th note in the suspended chord and add the b7th note, it will be considered a sus7 chord. As in Csus7, or C7sus4.

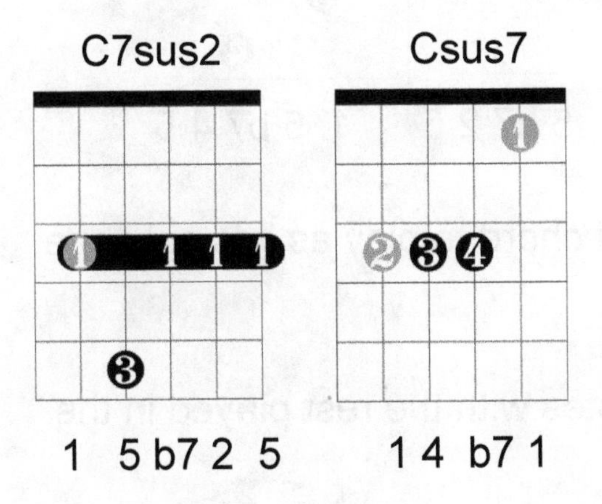

In the case of the C7sus2 chord we have barred all the notes on the 3rd fret except for the fifth note. That note, we moved to the fourth string 5th fret.

In the case of the Csus7 chord we eliminated the 5th note to make this chord easier to form in this position. In some cases, certain notes will be eliminated to make the chord easier to form in certain positions. As we only have four fingers.

Let's look at a few more suspended seventh chords:

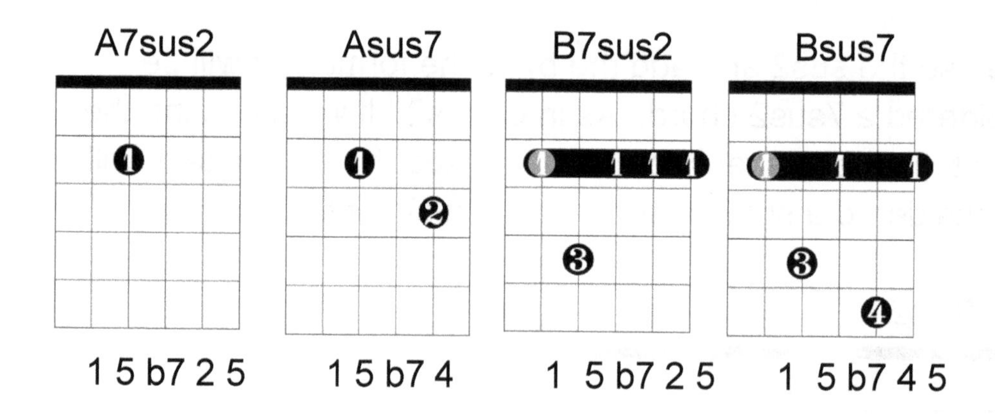

A7sus2 has got to be the easiest chord to play as it is only one finger on the 4th string 2nd fret.

Asus7 (or A7sus4) is only two notes with the rest played in the open position.

As where the B7sus2 & Bsus7 use a barre to the fifth string on the 2nd fret.

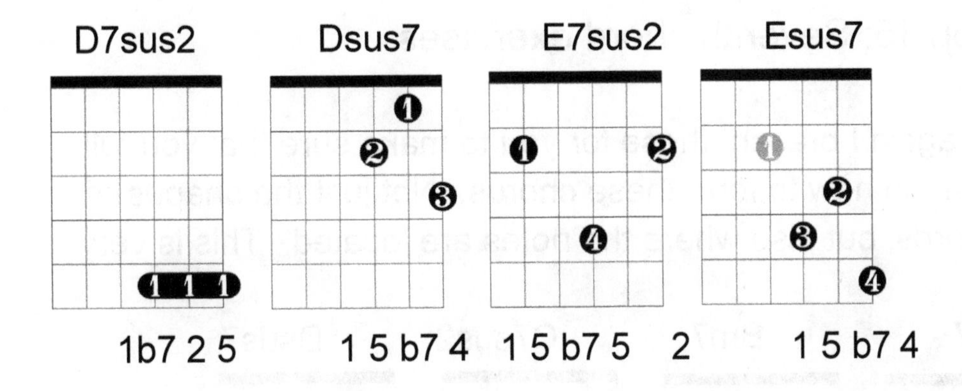

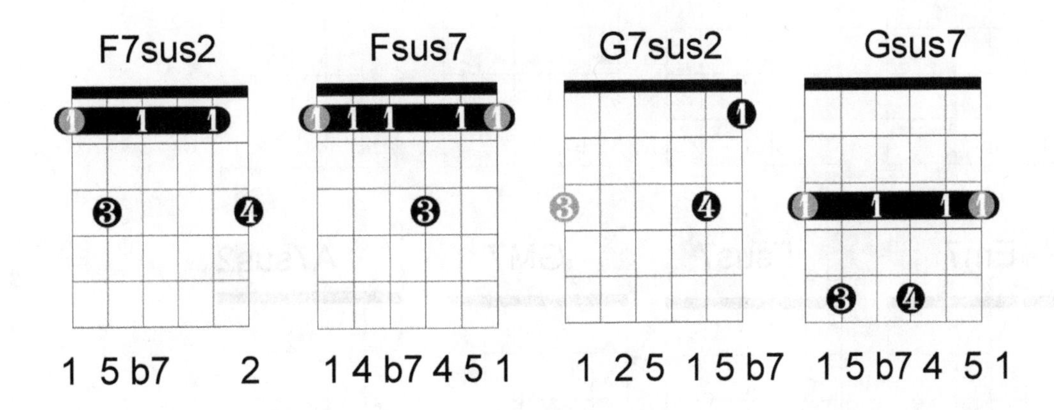

Once again we can see that all these chords have the correct formula. For the 7sus2 it is the 1 2 5 b7, and for the sus7 or 7sus4 chord it is the 1 4 5 b7.

You'll notice that as you study more chord theory beyond this book, chords will have different names. Like I said before, this can be confusing at first. The reason for this is because of inversions in the note formula.

Lesson 15: Seventh chord exercises

Once again I present these for you to make sure that you fully understand how to form these chords. Not just the shapes of the chords, but also where the notes are located. This is very

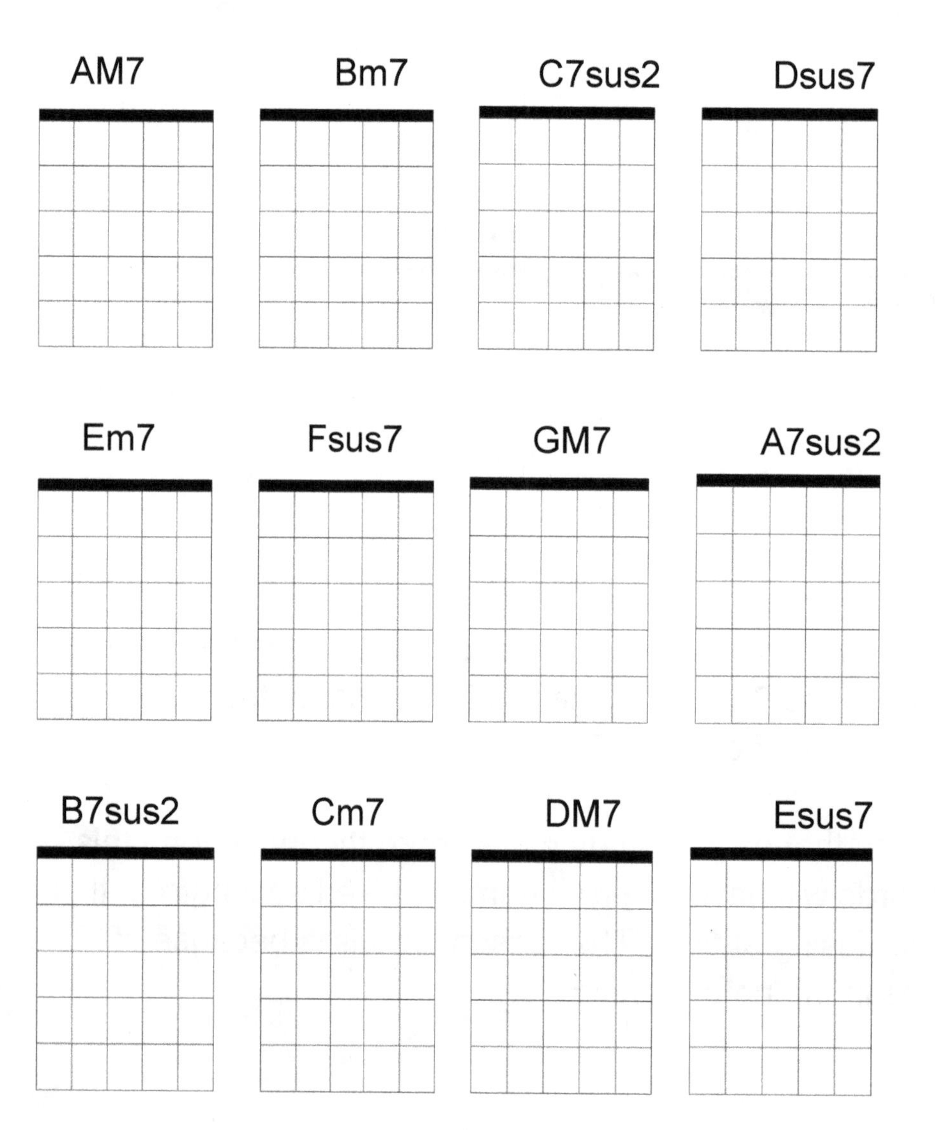

Chapter 3 summary

In chapter three we have extended our chord vocabulary to add the seventh chords. Major and minor. As well as adding the suspended chords and creating 7sus2 and sus7 chords.

Remember, that the sus7 can also be a 7sus4 chord name as well. This type of thing will become more common when you learn more extended chords.

First, we start with the major seventh chord. Which like the major sixth chord we just add the 7th note to extend the major triad. Major seventh: 1 3 5 7.

Second, we have the minor seventh chord. Similar to the major seventh, we just add the flat 7th note to extend the minor triad. Minor seventh: 1 b3 5 b7.

Third, we have the dominant seventh chord. This is a very unique chord as it consists of the flat seventh note added to the triad. Now the chord is not major, but dominant. 1 3 5 b7.

This is a great chord that has a very unique sound. It is very common in music and something to think about using if you decide to write your own music.

Fourth, we have the suspended seventh chords. This is where we mix the dominant 7th chord with the suspended chords. Since there are two types of suspended chords (sus2 and sus4) this allows us to create two more types of chords.

The 7sus2 chord, and the sus7 or 7sus4 chord.

With the 7sus2, we have a combination of the suspended second chord and the dominant 7th chord. With the sus7 chord, (or 7sus4) we have a combination of the suspended fourth chord and the dominant seventh chord.

7sus2 chord: 1 2 5 b7
sus7 chord: 1 4 5 b7

As I mentioned before, while progressing into the extended chord realm, you'll see very clearly that some of the chords have different names for them. The reason for this is because the notes within the chord can create multiple chords.

What I mean by this is that a certain chord can also be considered a different chord. Because of chord inversions. Which is something I'll talk about later in the training.

Fifth, we have seventh chord exercises. I present these because it is very important to know how to create these chords at any time you feel the need.

With these exercises, they also allow you to learn the notes on your guitar fretboard. Knowing the notes and where they are located on the fretboard can be a great asset to your guitar playing.

Of course a lot of guitar players play by ear and don't worry about knowing the notes, but if you're going to study books and training like this, I recommend you learn your notes.

Remember, all chords you study in this book along with other chords you learn later down the line, come from scales. And knowing exactly what notes are in each scale will help you to produce any chord within that key.

Seventh chords are very popular. More popular than the 6th chords. So I recommend you learn them very well. Study and know where the seventh note or flat seventh note is located This way you can add it to the triads or suspended chords.

Chapter 4 Ninth Chords

Lesson 16: Major ninth chords

When it comes to creating the major ninth chord, we just add the 9th note to the major seventh chord that we learned in the previous chapter. Real simple when you think about it.

The thing that is unique about the 9th chord and the rest we'll learn in this book, is that we need to take these notes from the second octave. One octave is 1-8 notes. So to add the 9th we grab it from the second octave past the 8th note.

To make this easier to create, all we need to do is remember that the notes repeat themselves after the first octave. Since the 8 and 1 are the same note, then that means that the 9th note will be the same as the 2nd.

C major scale: C D E F G A B C D etc.
1 2 3 4 5 6 7 8 9

This allows us to take the 2nd note and use it to play the 9th chord. Now we can use the 2nd note for two types of chords. The sus2 chord, as well as the ninth chord. Both major and minor.

Knowing what the chord formula for the major ninth chord is really easy because we already know what the chord formula for the major 7th. Like I said, we just add the ninth note to the formula.

Example: AM9= 1 3 5 7 9

Let's look at some major ninth chords:

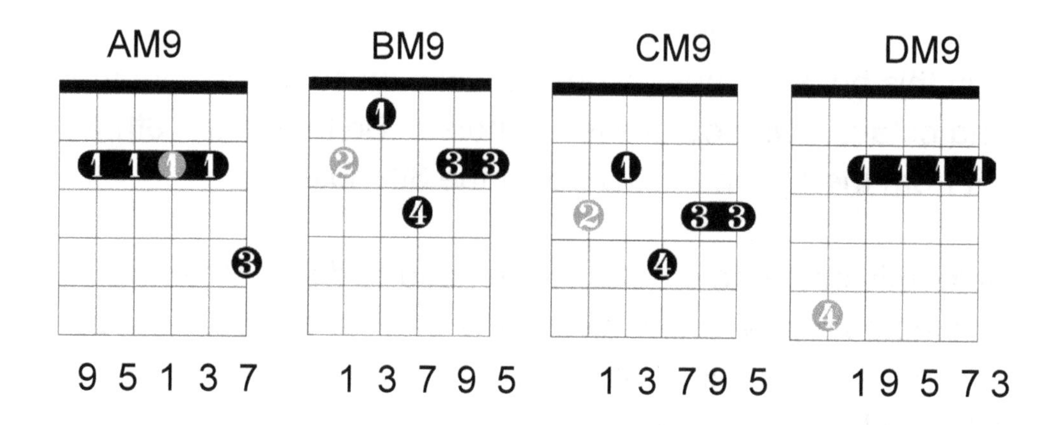

Just like with all the other chords presented in the previous lessons, these all have the correct chord formula in the chords.

AM9 can be formed with a partial barre at the 2nd fret and the 7th note added on the 4th.

BM9 can be formed with a partial barre on the 2nd fret single notes on the fifth, fourth, and third strings.

CM9 can be played with the same exact note placement as the BM9, you just move up a fret.

And DM9 can be formed quite easily with a barre on the 2nd fret up to the fourth string with the root note (the 1) added on the 5th fret fifth string.

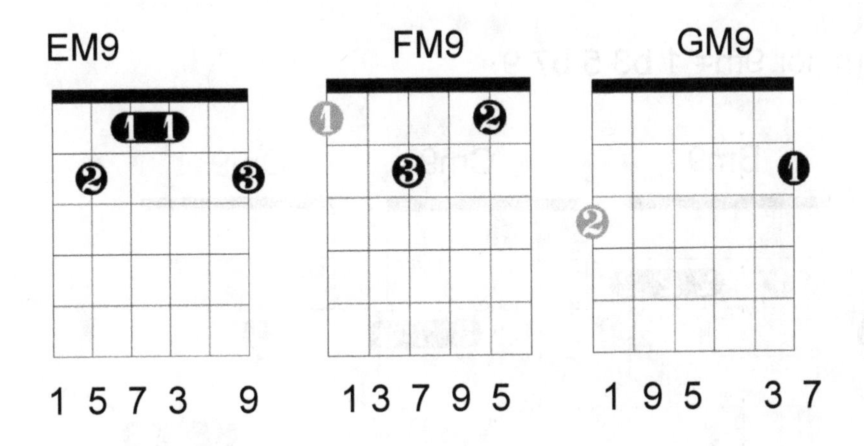

EM9 has a partial barre on the 1st fret adding a couple notes on the 2nd fret of the fifth and first strings.

FM9 is easy to form with just three fretted notes on 1st and 2nd frets of the sixth, fifth, and second strings.

GM9 can easily be formed by just fretting two notes on the 3rd and 2nd frets of the sixth and first strings.

Practice these chords and get to know how to form them.

Lesson 17: Minor ninth chords

Same as before with the major ninth, we just add the 9th note to the minor 7th chord. Now our chord formula will have the flat 3rd and the flat 7th notes. This will make it sound quite different from its major counterpart.

Example: A minor 9th= 1 b3 5 b7 9

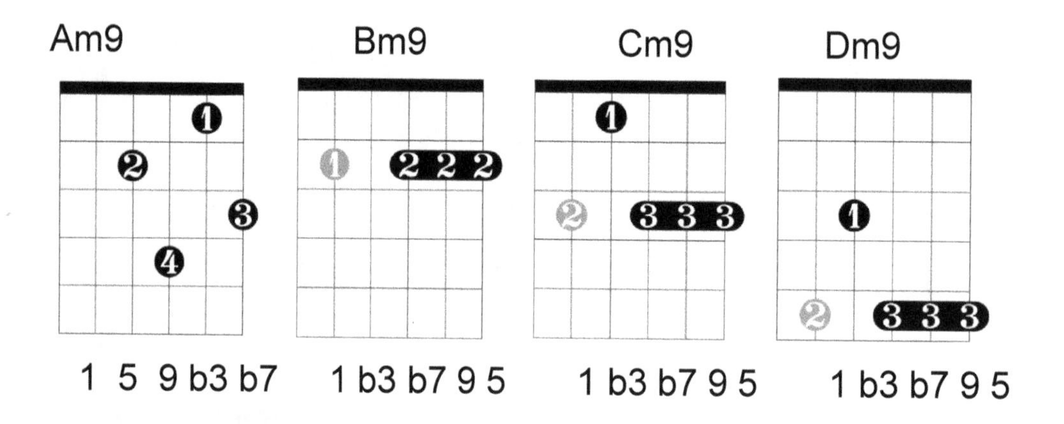

We can see from the chord chart diagrams that all these chords have the correct m9th formula.

Am9 is four individual notes on four strings with a bit of a stretch using all four fingers.

Bm9 uses a simple barre on the second fret skipping over the fourth string.

Cm9 uses a barre on the 3rd fret with a couple notes added on the fifth and fourth strings.

Dm9 can be formed the same way as the Cm9 chord, we just move everything up two frets.

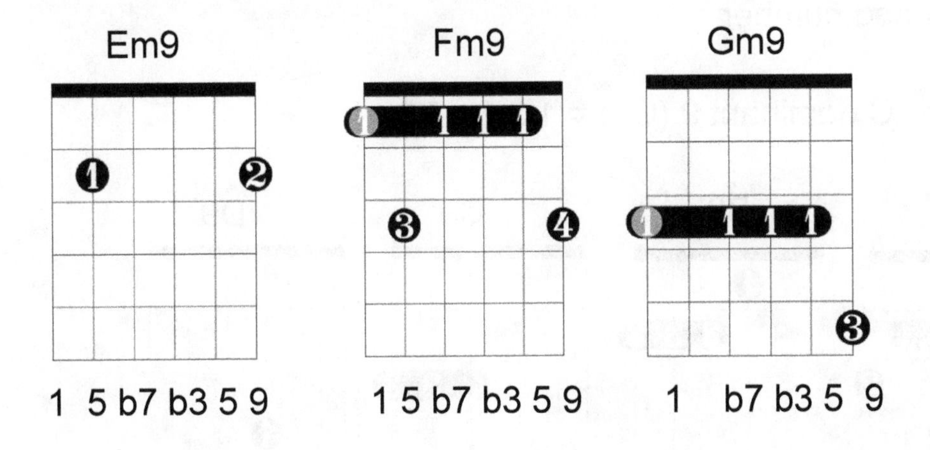

Em9 uses only two fretted notes with the rest being open.

Fm9 is the same, we just move the notes down a fret and add a barre on the 1st fret.

Gm9 is almost the same thing as well. We just move everything down two frets and eliminate a note.

Like the other chords presented in this chapter, the chord all have the m9th chord formula. 1 b3 5 b7 9. See if you can find these chords in other areas of the fretboard.

Lesson 18: Dominant ninth chords

The dominant ninth chords use the same concept as the major and minor ninths. We just add the 9th note to the dominant 7th chord. Since it is based off of the dominant 7th, it will just be the letter and number.

Example: C dominant 9 (C9) = 1 3 5 b7 9

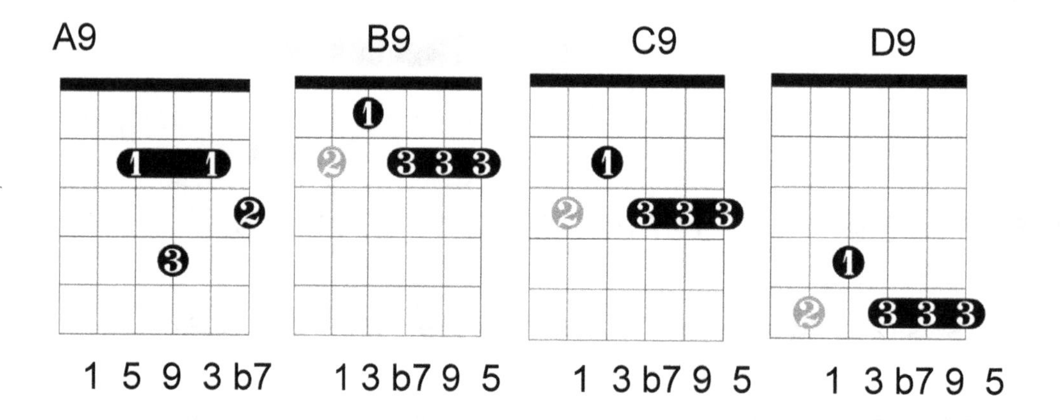

Once again, we can see that these chords have the correct chord formula. As well as the B9, C9, and D9 all have them in the same order.

The A9 chord is a little different in the fact that the flat 7th note is located on the 3rd fret of the first string.

The dominant ninth chord can also be thought of as a major ninth flat seven chord. This is because it has a natural third in it. But because it is built off of the dominant 7th chord, it is called a dominant ninth chord.

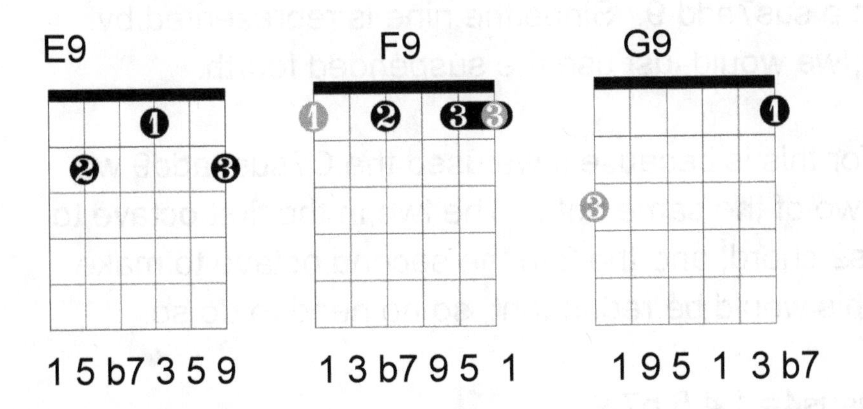

The E9 can be formed easily by fretting just three notes on the first, third, and fourth strings.

The F9 notes are all located on the first fret. But has a couple open notes. So this one can be a bit tricky to form.

And the G9 chord is the easiest as it just frets two notes with the rest of them being played open.

You will see (as I've said before) that this chord has multiple names. A ninth chord, A major ninth flat seven chord, or it could even be considered a dominant add nine chord.

Don't let this confuse you when learning these chords.

Lesson 19: Suspended ninth chords

Once again, we just mix and match to create new chords. Here we just add the ninth note to the suspended seventh chords. We can have a sus7add 9. Since the nine is represented by the 2nd note, we would just use the suspended fourth.

The reason for this is because if we used the C7sus2add9 we would have two of the same note. The two in the first octave to make the sus2 chord, and the 2 in the second octave to make the ninth. This would be redundant, so no need to do so.

Example: C9sus4= 1 4 5 b7 9

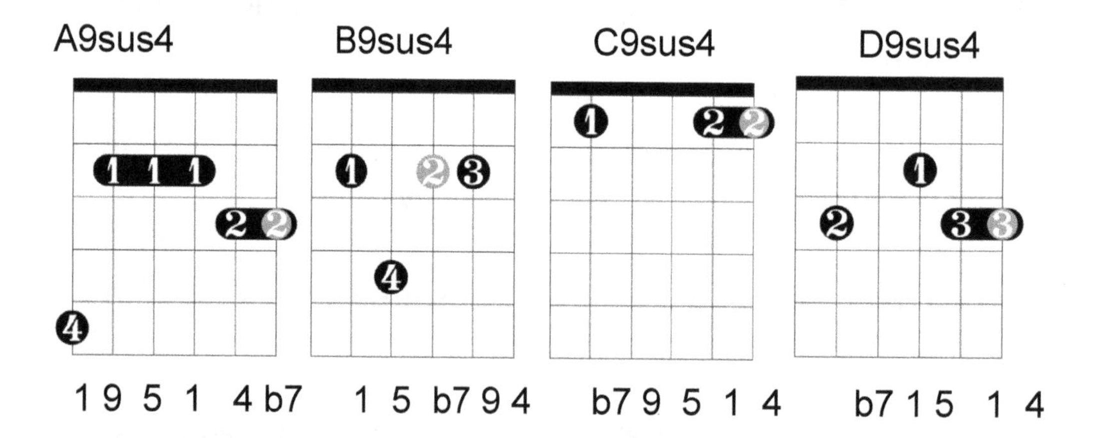

Once again we can see that all these chords have the 9sus4 chord formula notes. The 1 4 5 b7 9. This chord can also be known as a sus4add9. Same chord, just different names.

Remember, you're going to run into this kind of thing as you learn more complex extended chords. This is the reason why thousands of chords can be created on the guitar.

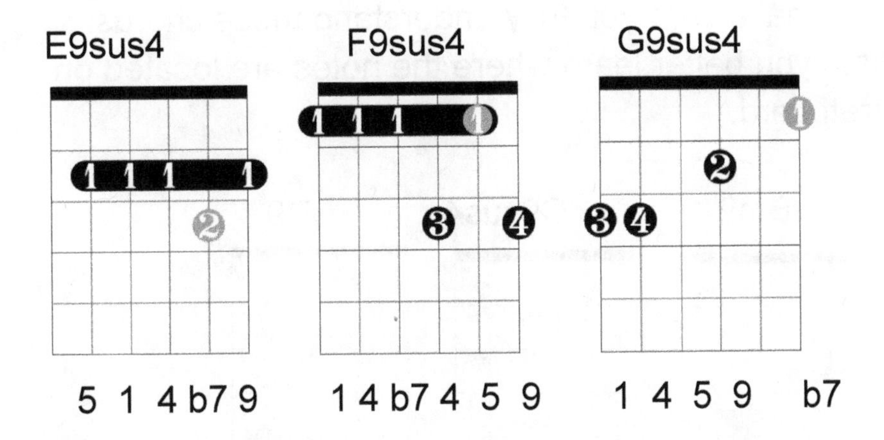

5 1 4 b7 9 1 4 b7 4 5 9 1 4 5 9 b7

These chords all have the correct formula as well. The E and F chords use a barre and the G chord needs to skip the second string. As this is a B note and it's not in the formula. So that would be a good chord to play the strings individually.

You'll notice this as well when you learn more complex chords. Some will sound great strumming, and some will sound better with the notes played individually.

You will also notice that as you learn more extended chords, one of the notes is sometimes eliminated. This is because we only have four fingers. So it would be quite impossible to play a chord that has 6 or more notes.

Lesson 20: Ninth chord exercises

Once again we come to the exercise part of this chapter. This will help you to make sure you fully understand these chords. As well as help you better learn where the notes are located on your guitar fretboard.

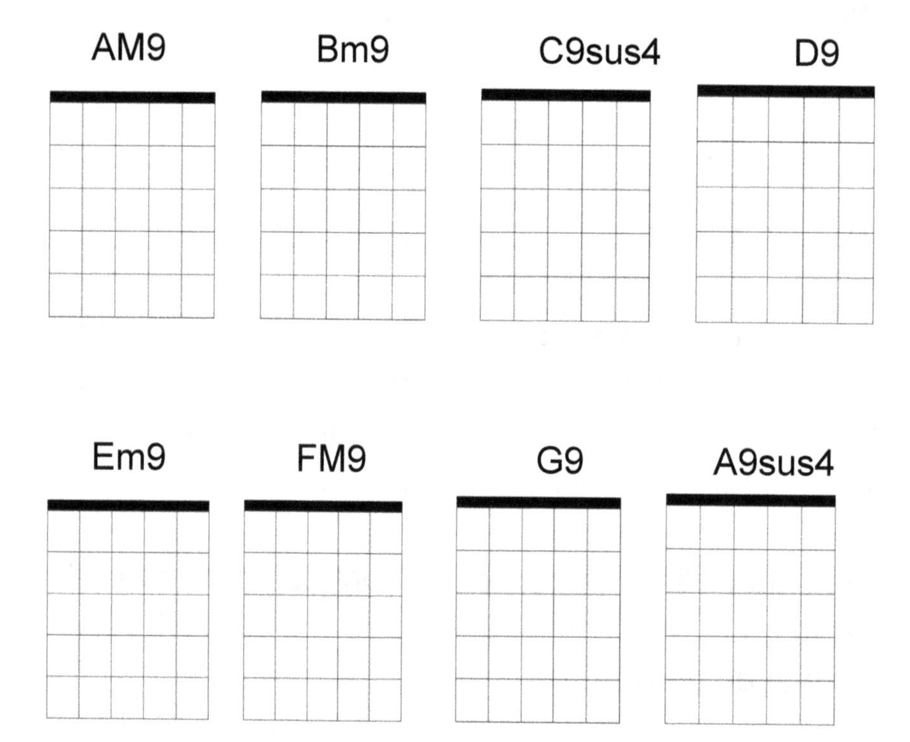

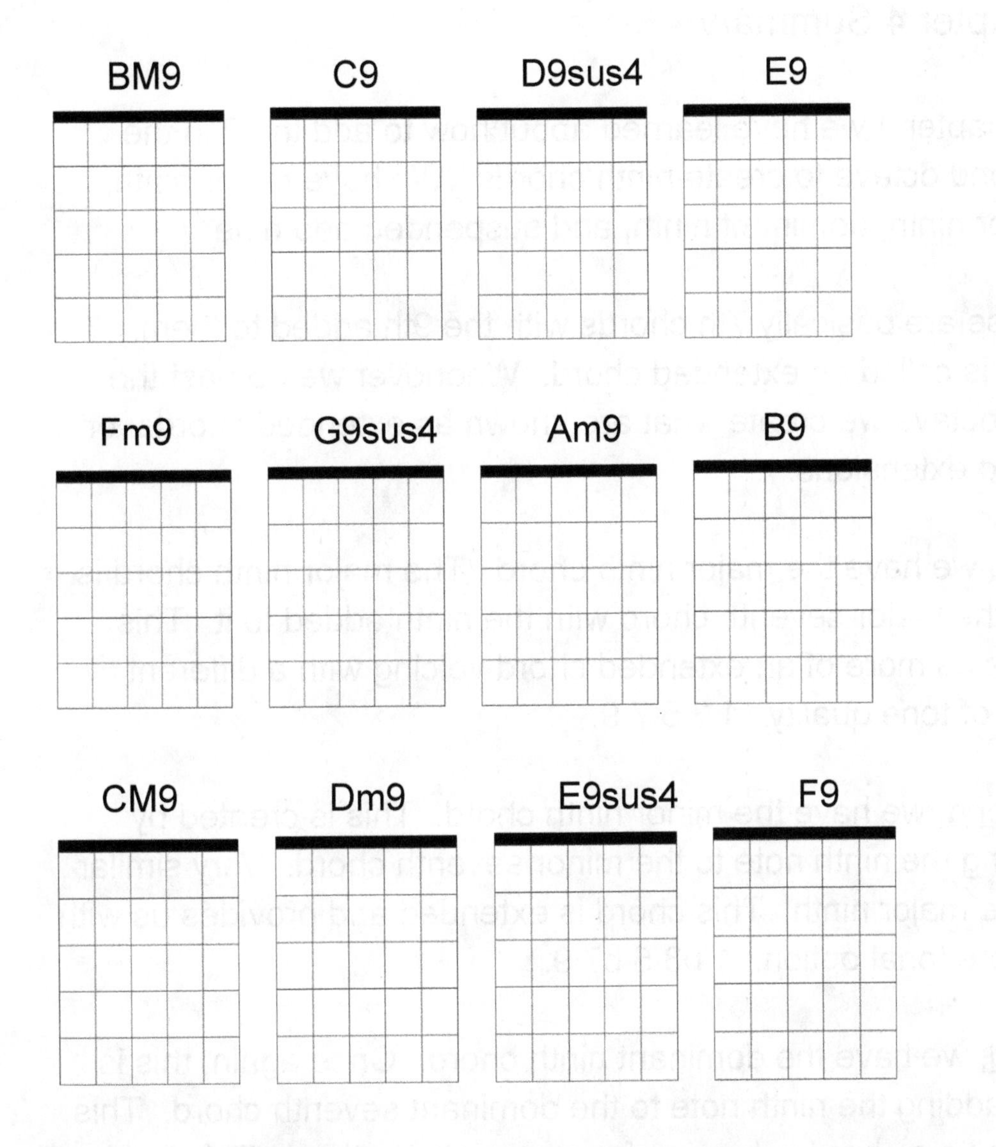

Remember, these are just a few ninth chords. You can actually create more if you just know the notes. You can create minor dominant ninth chords, augmented ninth chords, diminished ninth chords, etc. So work on creating these as well.

Chapter 4 Summary

In chapter 4 we have learned about how to add the 2 in the second octave to create ninth chords. We have major ninth, minor ninth, dominant ninth, and suspended add nine.

These are basically 7th chords with the 9th added to them. This is called an extended chord. Whenever we go past the first octave we create what are known as extended chords, or chord extensions.

First, we have the major ninth chord. The major ninth chord is like the major seventh chord with the ninth added to it. This gives us more of an extended chord voicing with a different type of tone quality. 1 3 5 7 9.

Second, we have the minor ninth chord. This is created by adding the ninth note to the minor seventh chord. Very similar to the major ninth, This chord is extended and provides us with a more tonal option. 1 b3 5 b7 9.

Third, we have the dominant ninth chord. Once again, this is just adding the ninth note to the dominant seventh chord. This gives us a chord extension for more color options. This is what these types of chords are designed for.

Fourth, we have a suspended ninth chord. This is the same concept. We add the ninth to the suspended chord. This creates a 9sus chord, or a susadd9 chord.

Since the ninth note is represented by the 2 in the second octave, we don't want to create a sus2 add9 because we would just be adding another 2 to the chord, and that would be redundant, so that wouldn't work.

So we leave that suspended chord out and add the ninth note to the suspended fourth. Now we have a four and a two in the chord. This creates the suspended ninth chord.

And since this is an extension past the dominant seventh chord, we want to have that flat seven in there as well. The chord formula for this chord will be 1 4 5 b7 9.

Fifth, we have ninth chord exercises. Chord chart diagrams that give us an opportunity to write these chords out. I present this at the end of every chapter. I recommend you use them to make sure you fully understand these chords.

These exercises will also be helpful in learning exactly where the notes in the chord formula are located. The more about this information you know, the faster you'll be able to create these chords.

Chapter 5 Eleventh chords

Lesson 21: Major eleventh chords

Like I said before, these are extension chords or considered chord extensions. And the next chord extension will be the eleventh chord. Here we look at the major eleventh chord.

This chord will consist of the notes 1 3 5 7 9 11. If the 2 in the second octave represents the 9, then what note in the second octave represents the eleven?

That's correct, the 4. So basically, the eleventh chord is a major seventh chord with two note extensions. The nine and eleven.

If we have a CM11 chord, we just look at the CM7 and add two more notes. 1 3 5 7 9 11. C E G B D F.

Pretty easy right?

Now since we have six notes and only four fingers, one of these notes needs to be eliminated to form it on the guitar. In this case, we will eliminate the ninth note. So let's look at some major eleven chords with a 1 3 5 7 11.

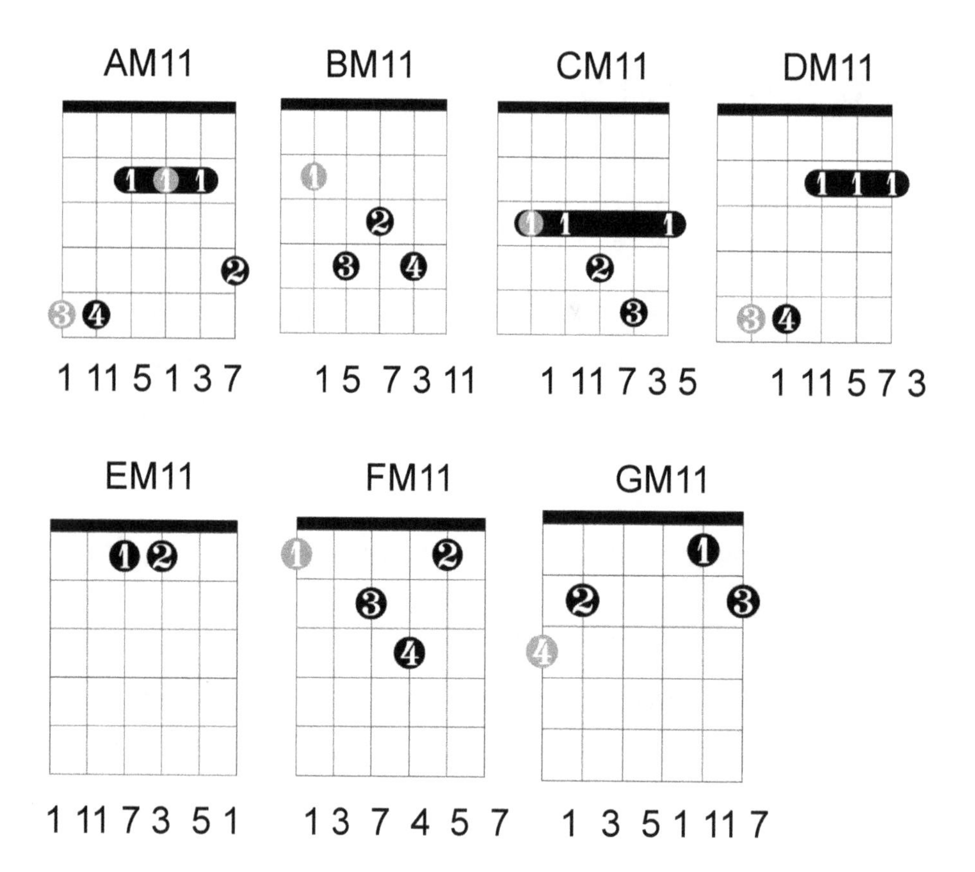

As we can see, each one of these chords have the correct chord formula for the M711th chord. Minus the 9th note. This is so we can actually form the chord on the guitar. In the case of certain chords, notes are sometimes eliminated.

This makes the chords easier to form and gives them a more unique emotional voicing. Remember, guitar chords are like shades of color. Your goal is to have different shades like an artist who paints.

Lesson 22: Minor eleventh chords

With the minor eleventh chord we do the same thing as we did with the major eleventh chord. We add the eleventh note to the minor seventh. And once again, we will eliminate the ninth note for easier fingering on the guitar.

So now we have a minor eleventh chord that consists of the chord formula 1 b3 5 b7 11. In the example of the Cm11 we will use the notes C Eb G Bb F.

This as well as the major eleventh chord can also be considered a seven add eleven chord. Major seven add eleven, and minor seven add 11.

Since we already know the minor seventh chord, all we need to do is add the eleven. Let's take a look at some minor eleventh chords.

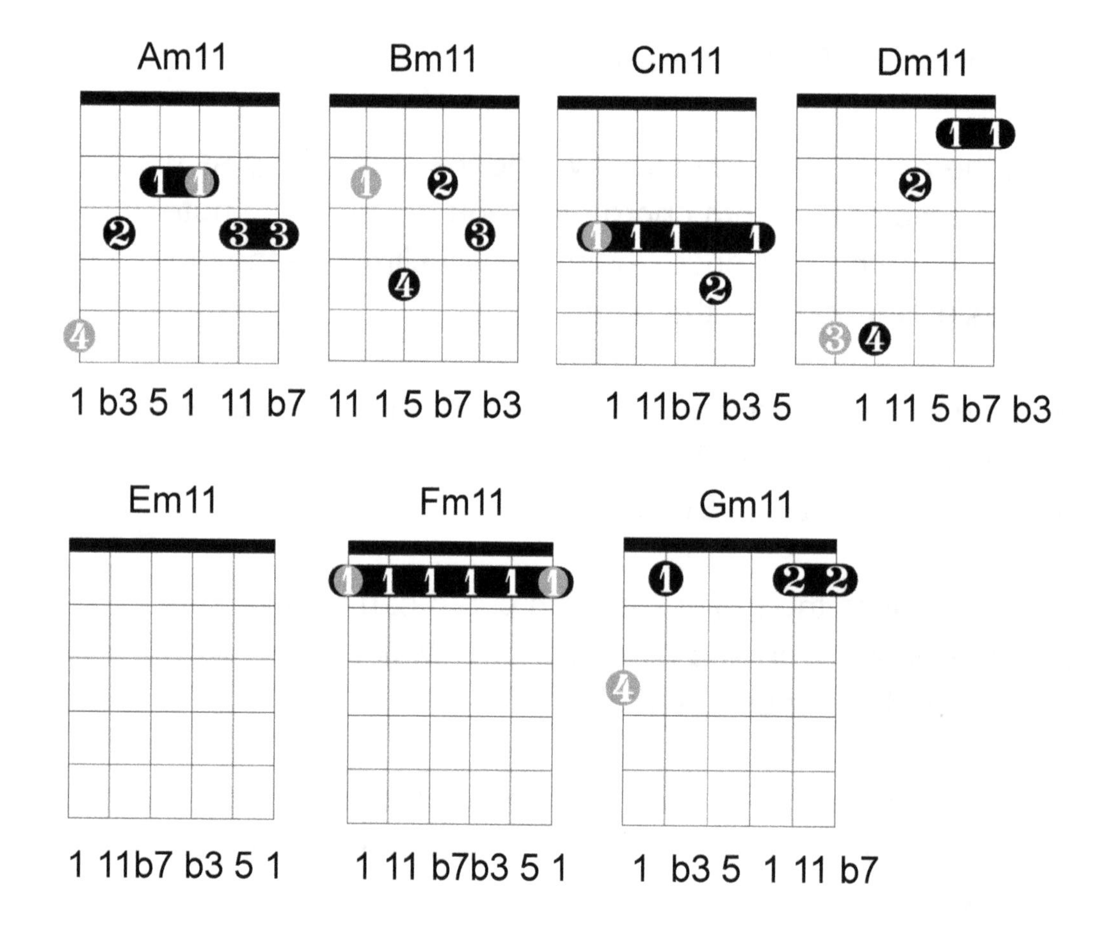

Like all the chords before, they all have the correct chord formula. 1 b3 5 b7 11. The Em11 is the easiest chord you'll ever play because all the notes line up to be open. Great!

Remember, the eleventh chords are created by adding the 4th to the seventh. Seven plus four equals eleven. And the 3rd and 7th notes will be flattened in the minor eleventh chord.

Lesson 23: Dominant eleventh chords

This chord is similar to the minor eleventh chord except with this chord we will use the natural third note. Just like with the dominant seventh. And once again, we are just adding the eleventh note to the dominant seventh chord.

This makes it easy to understand as well as form. If you know your dominant seventh chord, then making the chord dominant eleventh should be easy as you are just adding the eleventh note.

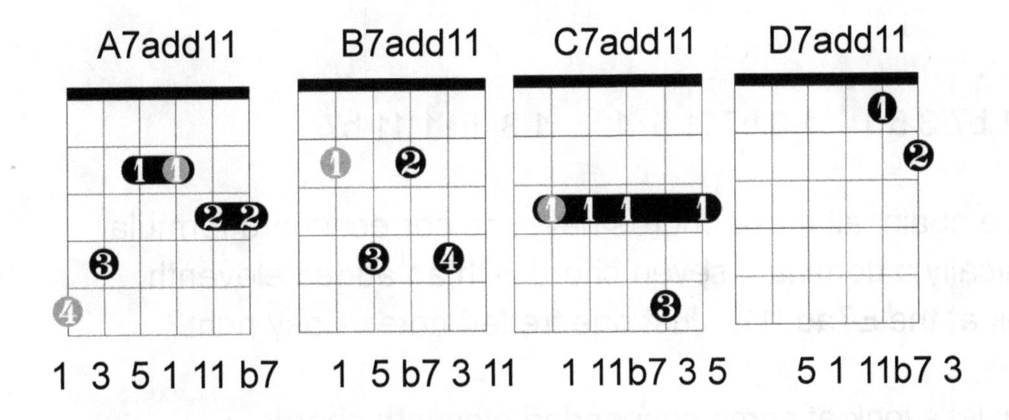

Just like before with the major and minor eleventh chords, we have eliminated the ninth note. Also, similar to the major 11th, we have the natural third. But with the dominant 11th, we've flattened the 7th note. Dominant 7 add 11.

Can you see how easy these chords are to form once you know the seventh chords? We are just taking that chord and adding a note. Technically the ninth note as well, but it makes it a little difficult to form with only four fingers.

So we eliminate that note for easier playability.

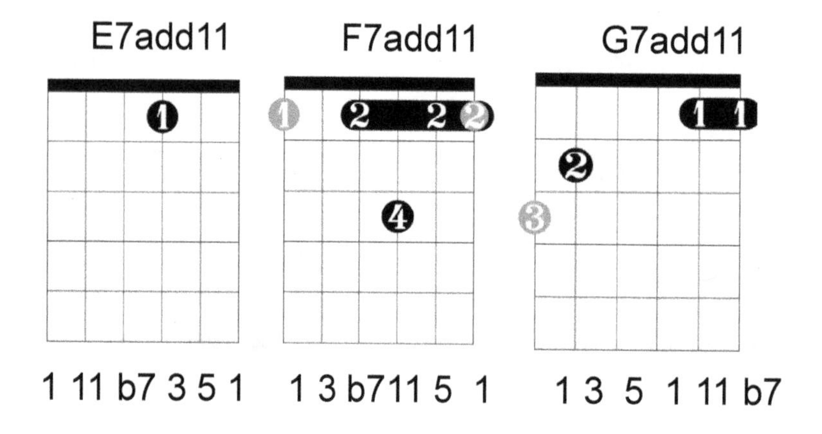

Once again, all these chords have the correct chord formula. Basically a dominant seven chord with an added eleventh. Look at the E7add11. Just one fretted note. Easy right?

Now let's look at some suspended eleventh chords.

Lesson 24: Suspended eleventh chords

Just like before with the suspended ninth chords, we add the eleventh and get a suspended eleventh chord. We move the third note over to create the sus and add the eleventh.

Now since the 11th is represented by a 4 in the second octave (same note is in the first) we don't want to use the sus4 add 11 because we would be putting in two fours in the chord formula which would be redundant.

So instead, just like with the ninth (represented by a 2) we will use the sus2 and then add the eleventh. For the sus9 we use the 4 and for the sus11 we will use the 2. This way we don't have multiple notes in the chord formula.

Also, to make the chord easier to form on the guitar because we only have four fingers we will take out the 7th note. This will give us a 4 note chord formula and be exactly what it says it is. A sus2add11. 1 2 5 11.

Now let's look at some sus2add11 chords.

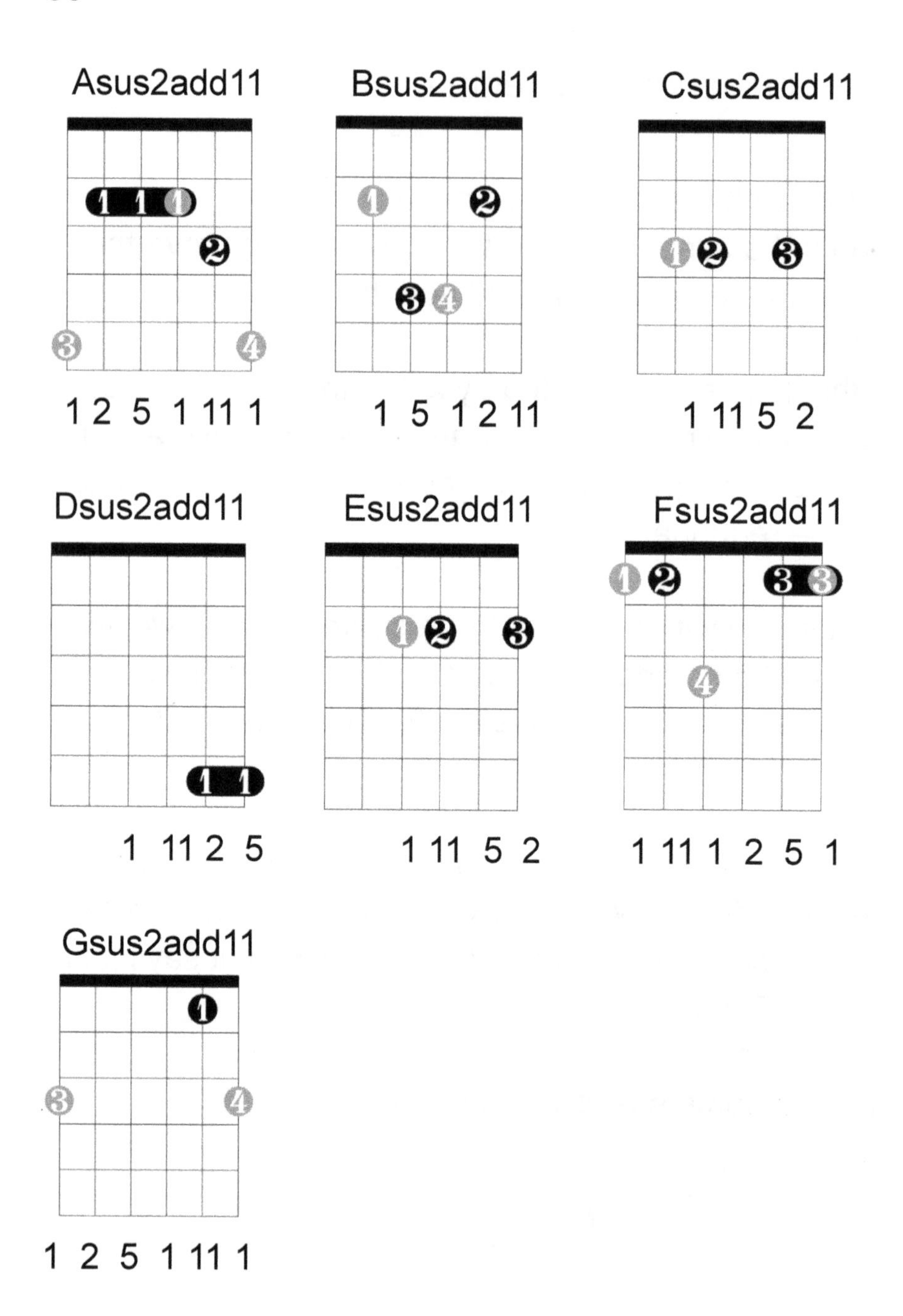

These chords will add to your guitar chord vocabulary.

Lesson 25: Eleventh chord exercises

Eleventh chords are nice chords to play in certain situations where you want to add suspense. Be sure to write these in the chord charts below. It will help you to know these chords and the notes within them better.

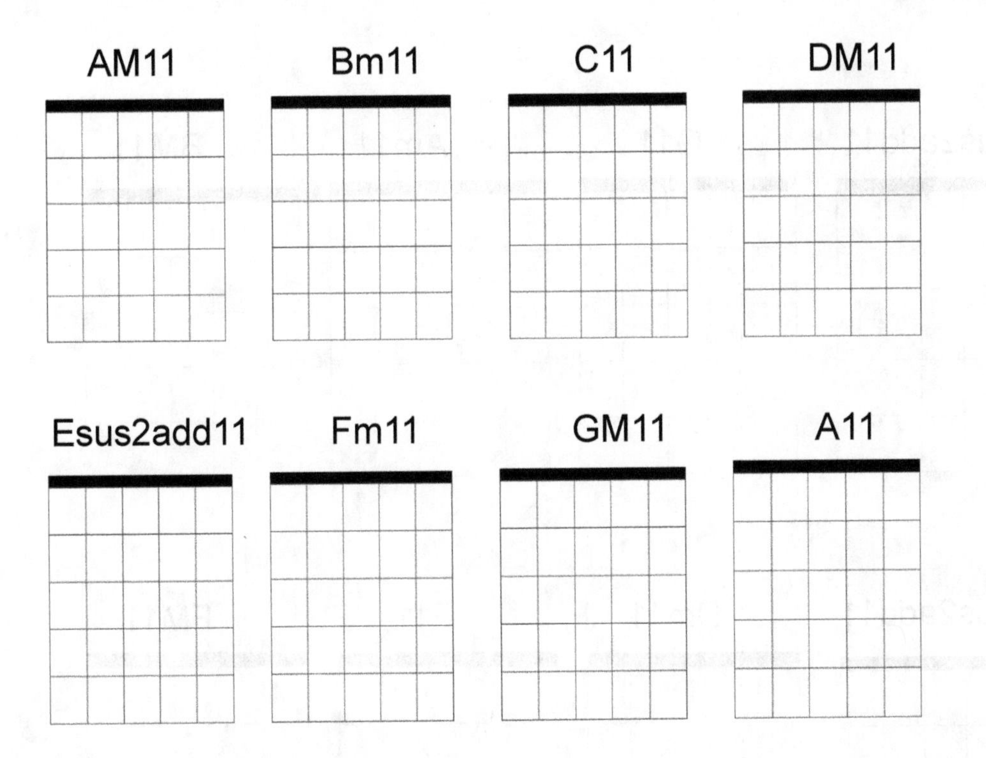

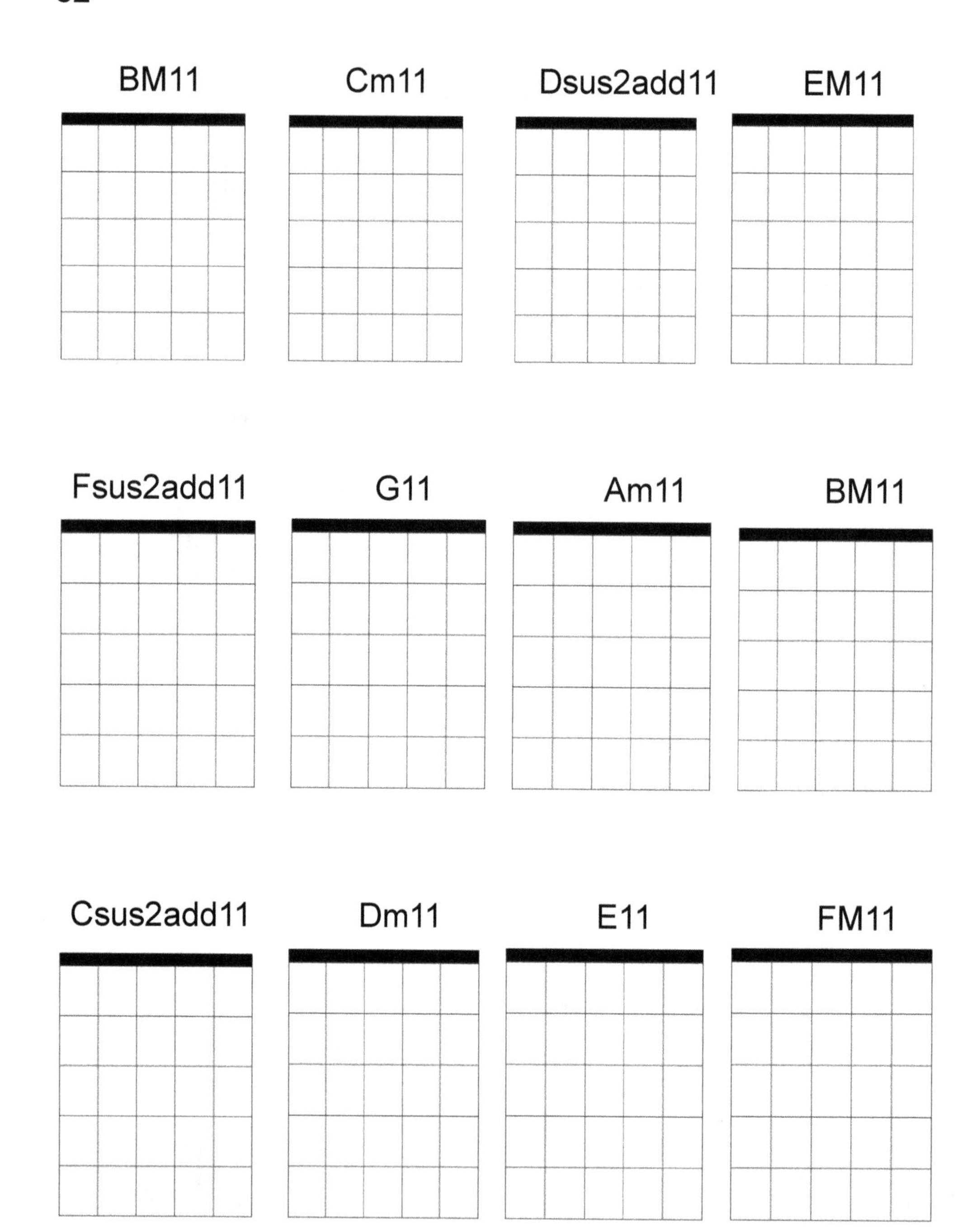
BM11
Cm11
Dsus2add11
EM11
Fsus2add11
G11
Am11
BM11
Csus2add11
Dm11
E11
FM11

Chapter 5 Summary

In this chapter we have looked at the eleventh chords. Major, minor, dominant and suspended. You can also create eleventh augmented and diminished chords. I left those out to keep the book from being too long.

Although I know you can figure those out on your own if you just use the same theory as the suspended eleventh chords.

First, we have the major eleventh chords. In this case we just use the major seventh chord and add the eleventh note to it. Remember, the eleven is represented by the 4th note in the second octave.

Second, we have the minor eleventh chords. Same is with the major, except we add the eleventh note to the minor seventh chord. Remember, the minor eleventh will have the flat third and flat seventh notes.

Major eleven chords have the natural third and seventh, and minor eleventh chords have the flattened third and seventh. And for easier playability (since we only have four fingers) we will eliminate the ninth note.

Third, we have the dominant eleventh chord. Once again, really simple to create. We just take our dominant seventh chord and add the eleventh note to it. So now we have a chord formula of 1 3 5 b7 11.

Remember, the dominant eleventh will have the flat seventh note, but have a natural third note. This is what separates it from the major and minor eleventh chords.

Fourth, we have the suspended eleventh chord. In this case we create the sus2add11 chord. We use the sus2 instead of the sus4 so we don't have two 4's in the chord formula.

Just like the other eleventh chords, this is really easy to figure out as well. We just play the suspended second chord and add the eleventh note to it. 1 2 5 11.

Fifth, we have eleventh chord exercises. These are very important and will help you to fully understand these chords when you see them written out. Remember, music is a language and you want to be able to read and write it.

Chapter 6 Thirteenth chords

Lesson 26: Major thirteenth chords

Now we come to the thirteenth chords. These are a nice addition to our chord vocabulary and will be useful in certain situations as well. And once again, we use the major seventh chord and just add the thirteenth note to it. 1 3 5 7 13.

Now, if the eleventh note is represented by the 4th in the second octave, what note represents the thirteenth?

That's correct, the 6. Since we now have a six and a seven in the chord formula, we can call it a thirteenth chord. This is because when you put 6 and 7 together you get 13.

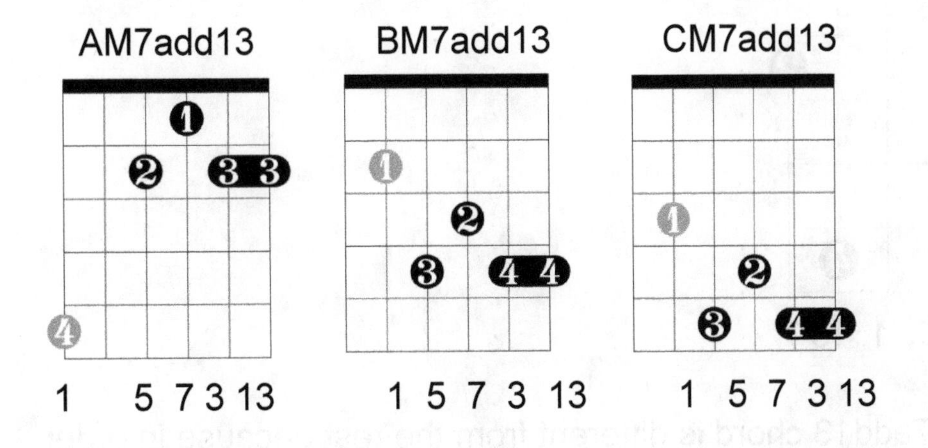

As we can see from the chord formulas on the previous page, they all have the correct chord formula. 1 3 5 7 13.

Let's look at some more major 13 chords.

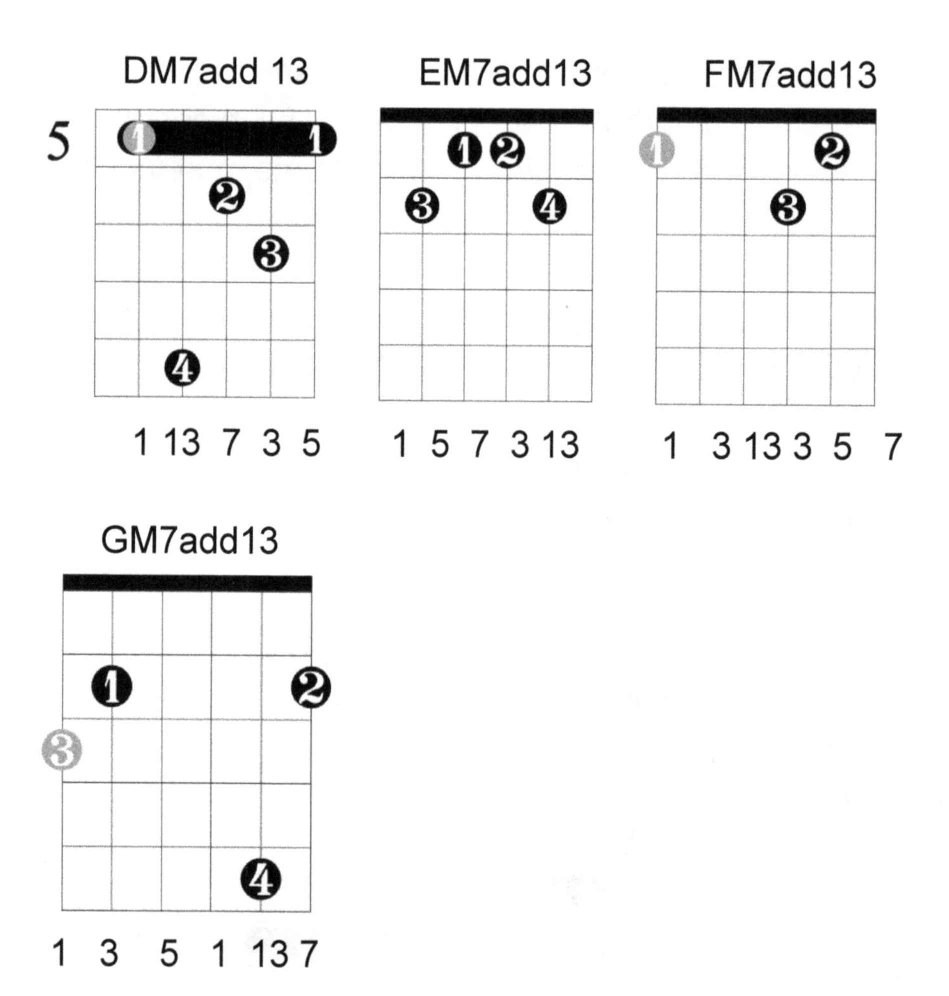

The DM7add13 chord is different from the rest because in order to form this particular chord we need to move up the fretboard to the 5th fret.

To play this chord correctly we need to use a barre to the fifth fret. This is considered a root five barre chord. These will be discussed later in the training. Barre chords are how you play chords further up the fretboard.

All the chords that I have shown you so far are all formed in the open position. As you can see with all the other M7add13 chords, they are all pretty easy to form.

Remember, the Major thirteenth chord can be considered major 13th, or major seven add thirteen. Two different names for the same chord. As I said before, you're going to run into this as you learn more extended chords.

Now let's look at some minor seven add thirteen chords.

Lesson 27: Minor thirteenth chords

Just like with the major thirteenth chords, all we need to do is add the thirteenth note to the minor seventh chord. And again, to make this easier to form we will eliminate the ninth note. So now we have a chord formula of 1 b3 5 b7 13

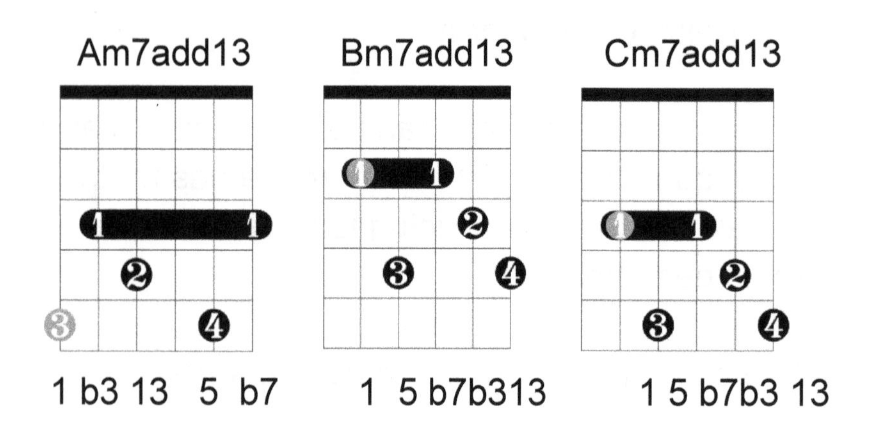

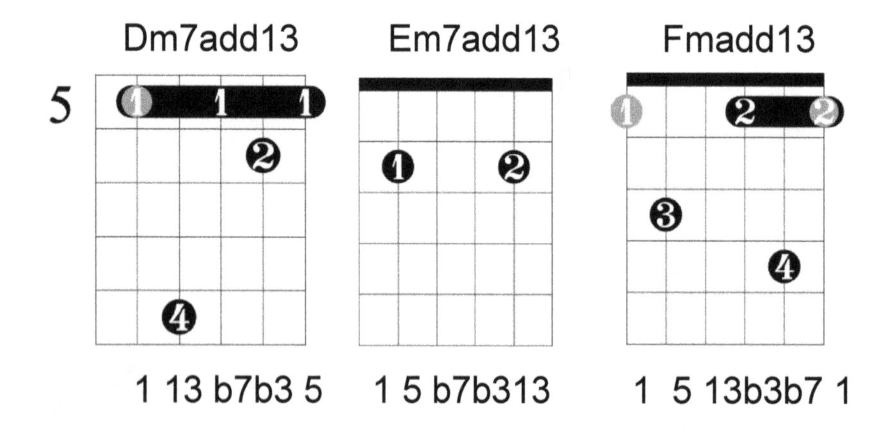

Once again, we can see that the Dm7add11 chord is at the 5th fret. This is because that's the easiest way to form this chord. Once the notes go past the first five frets in the chord chart, a number on the left represent the next five frets.

If the barre is within the first five frets, there will not be a number on the left to represent the frets. So even though some of the chords have a barre in them, they all reside within the first five frets that the chord chart represents.

Gm7add11

1 b3 5 1 13 b7

As before, we can see that all these chords have the correct chord formula. Remember, the thirteenth note is represented by the sixth in the second octave.

The Am13 chord has a barre like the Dm13, but is at the third fret.

Bm13 has a barre at the second fret.

The Cm13 is the same chord shape, just moved up a fret.

The Dm13 is moved up to the fifth fret so it needs a fret marker on the side to let us know the rest of the notes are located further up the fretboard.

The Em13 is really simple to form. Just two fretted notes on the second fret.

The Fm13 has a partial barre on the first fret and a bit of a stretch with the fourth finger.

The Gm13 chord doesn't have a barre in it, but like the Fm13 chord it has a bit of a stretch with the fourth finger.

Because of this stretch, some of these extended chords can be a bit tricky to play. I recommend you work daily on finger exercises to help condition your fingers to stretch.

Remember, the minor thirteenth chords will have a flat 3rd and a flat 7th in them.

Now let's look at dominant thirteenth chords. Do you remember what the dominant seventh chord formula is?

Lesson 28: Dominant thirteenth chords

Just like the minor seventh add thirteen chord, we just take the dominant seventh chord and do the same thing. With the minor seventh add thirteenth we have both b3rd and b7th notes. With the dominant thirteenth we just have the b7th.

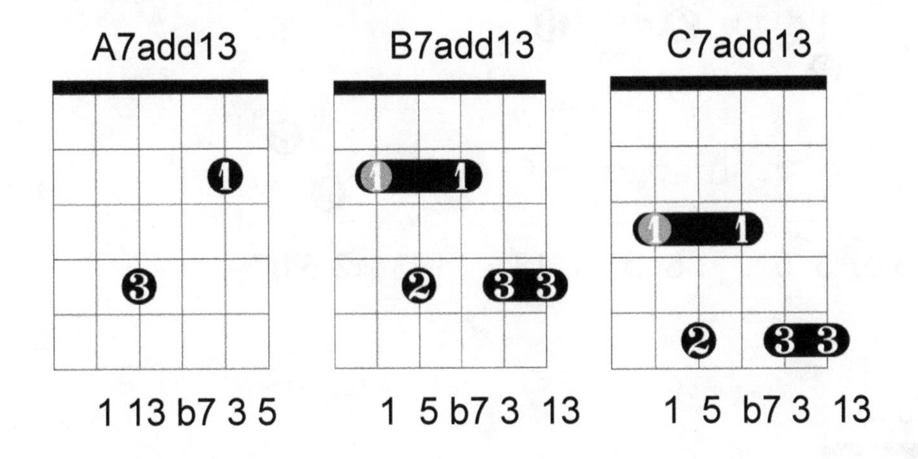

The A7add13 is easy to form with just two fretted notes.

The B7add13 has a partial barre on the second fret and another partial barre on the fourth fret.

The C7add13 is the same chord except you just move all the notes down a fret.

And once again, we can see that all the chords have the correct chord formula. These are the same as the minor7add13, we just keep the 3rd note natural.

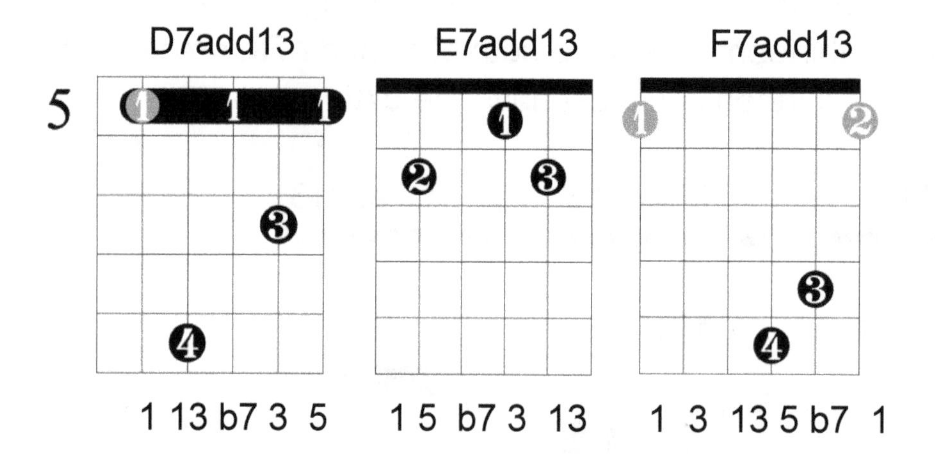

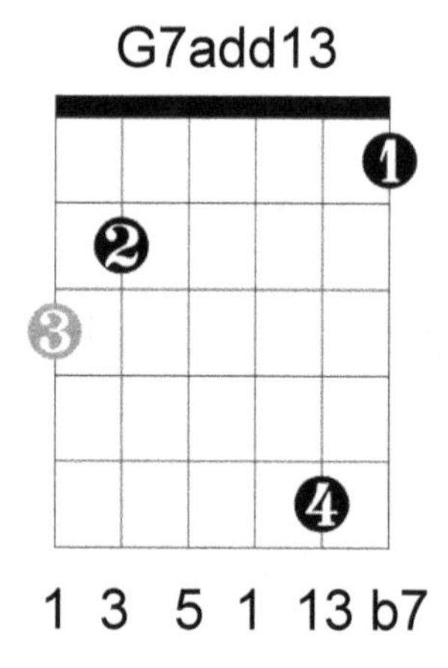

See how easy it is to create a whole new chord? We just keep the third in its natural position, or move it up one fret from the minor7add13 and we now have a dominant 7add13.

Lesson 29: Suspended thirteen chords

Just like the suspended 9th and 11th chords, we can do the same here. But since we are using the 6 to represent the 13 we can use both the sus2 and sus4 to create sus13 chords.

We can also do one of two things. We can create a sus2add13 chord, where we eliminate the 7th note. Or we can create a 7susadd13 chord where we include the 7th note. Technically the 13 is represented by the 6th note.

So for our purposes here, we will keep the 7th note and create the 7sus2add13 and 7sus4add13 chords. The chord formulas will be, 1 2 5 b7 13 and 1 4 5 b7 13.

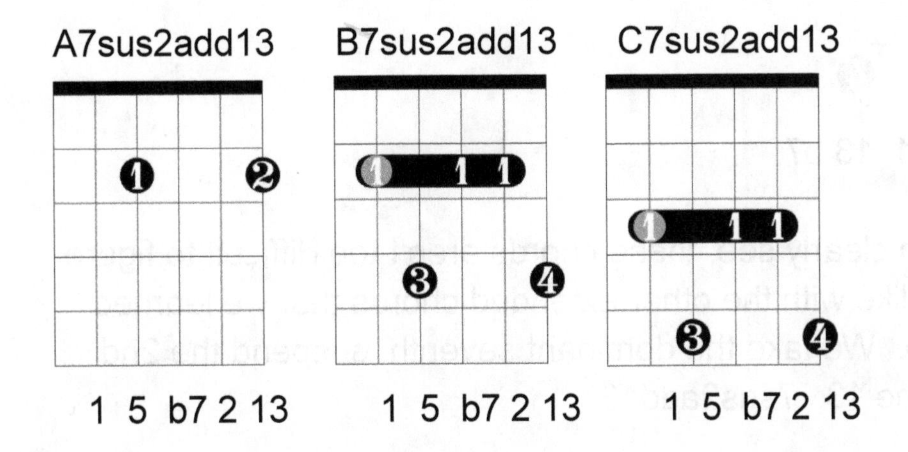

Remember, in the case of the 7susadd13 chords we will use the b7th note in the chord formula.

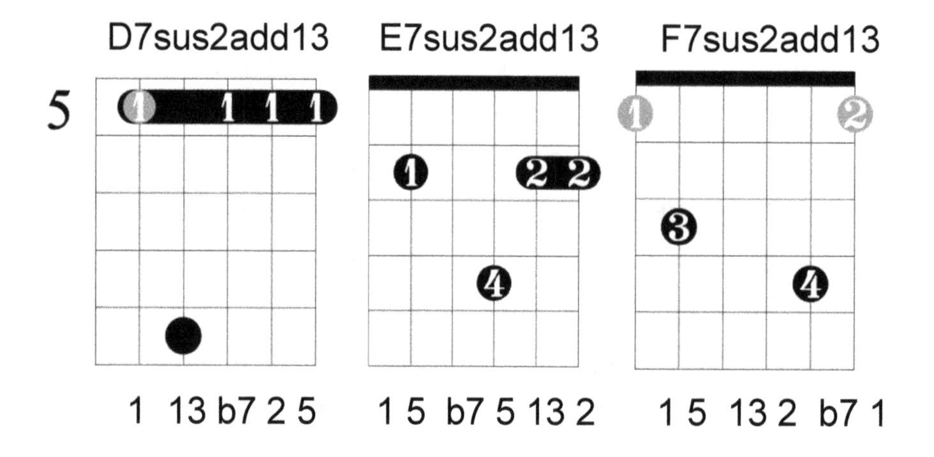

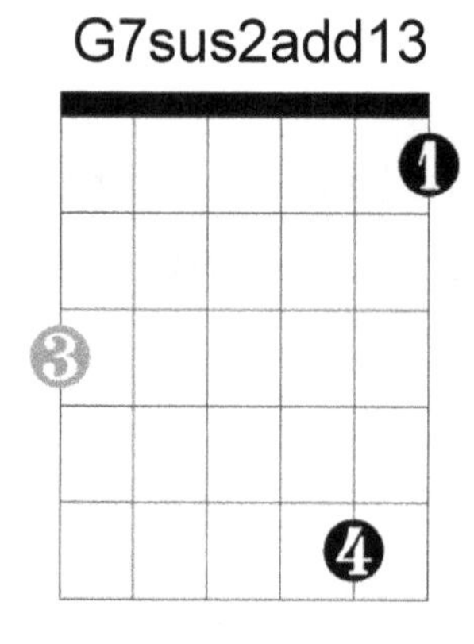

1 2 5 1 13 b7

As we can clearly see, these chords aren't too difficult to figure out. Just like with the other extended chords that we learned previously. We take the dominant seventh, suspend the 2nd and add the 13. 7sus2add13.

Now let's take a look at some 7sus4add13 chords.

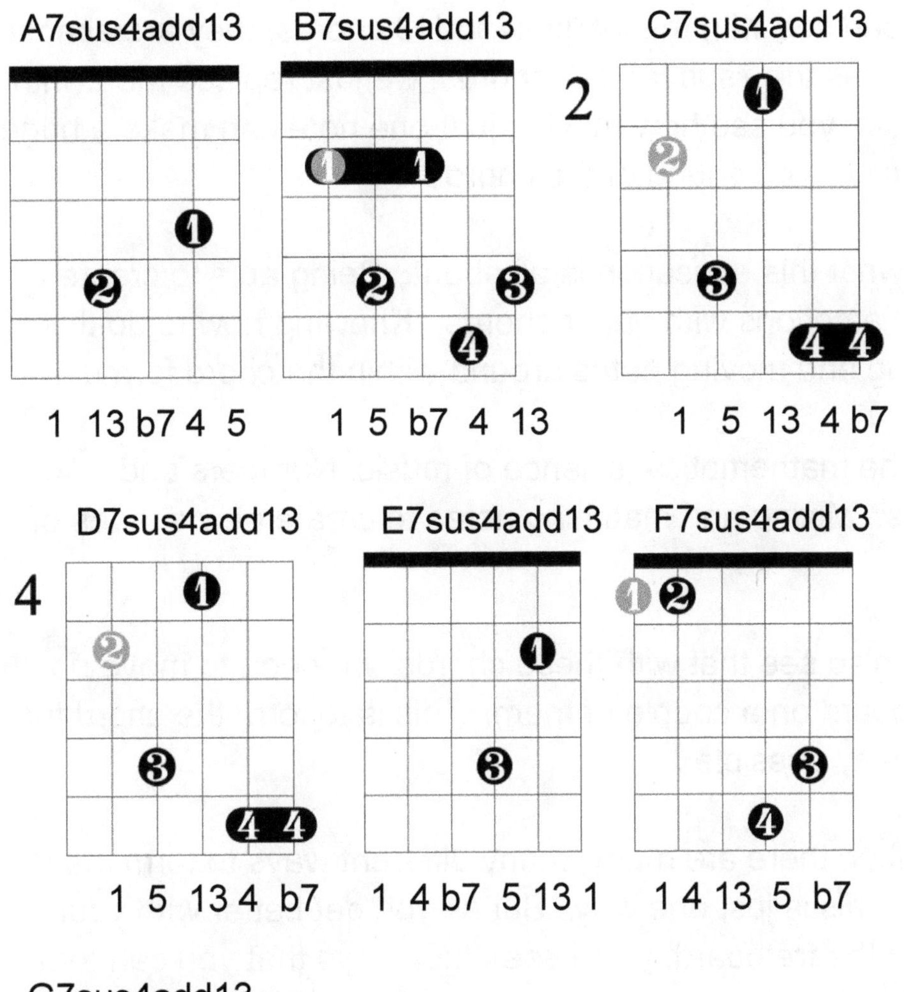

G7sus4add13

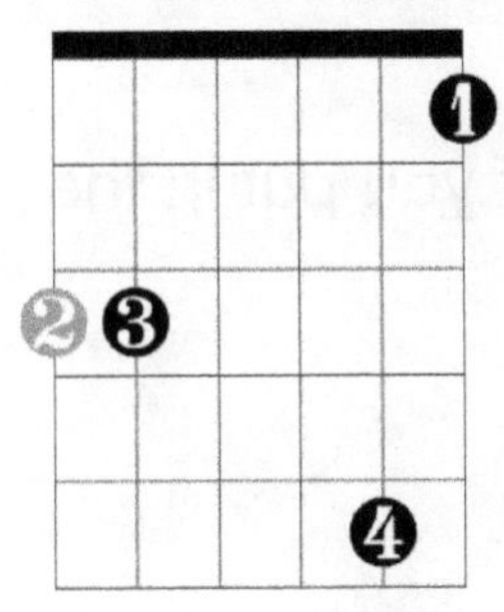

1 4 5 1 13 b7

As you can see with these 7sus4add13 chords, they are almost the same as the 7sus2add13 chords, we just replace the 2 with the 4. Can you see how moving just one note can make a huge difference on the sound of the chord?

That is what this education is all about. Being able to create different emotions with guitar chords. Knowing how to do this by adding and moving notes around within the chord formula.

This is the mathematical science of music. Numbers and formulas. Mixing and matching notes to create new shades of color.

We can also see that with these chords, we need to move up the fretboard on a couple of them. This is to form the chord the easiest way possible.

Remember, there are many, many different ways to form these chords. This is just one way. But as you get better with your notes on the fretboard, you'll see other ways that you can form these chords.

You just need to practice them to see that. But if you put in the effort, over time you will.

Lesson 30: Thirteenth chord exercises

I present these in each chapter for you to fully understand these chords. Since these are extended chords, they require a little bit more thinking to figure them out as they are only commonly used within certain styles of music.

What they offer, is the ability to see how chords are fully constructed.

AM13 Bm13 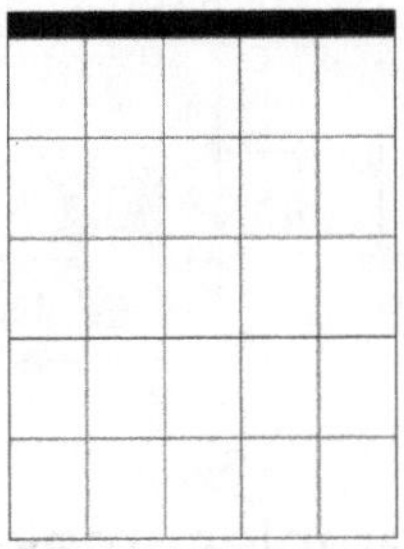 C7add13 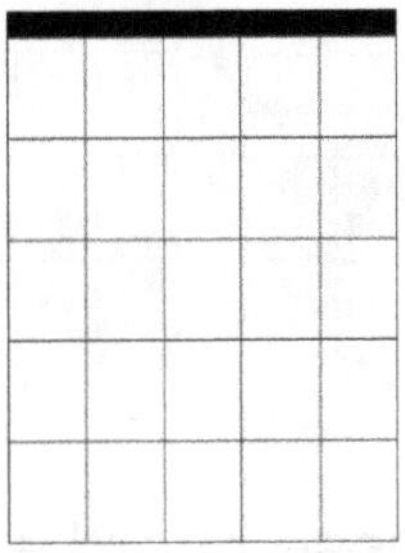 D7sus2add13

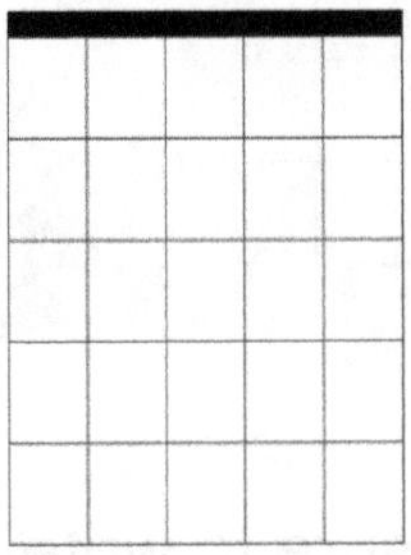

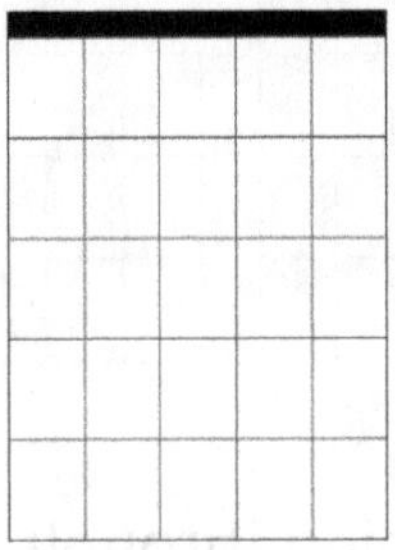

Em13 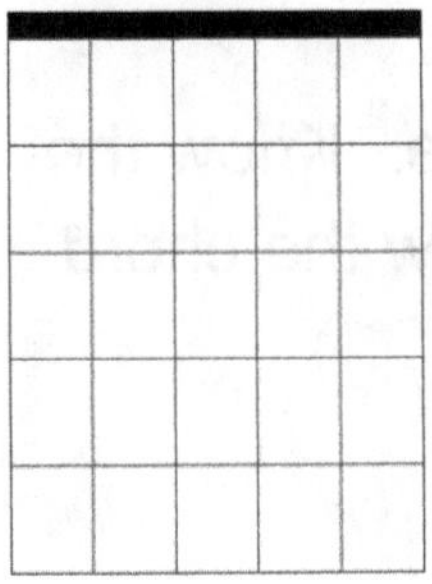 F7sus4add13 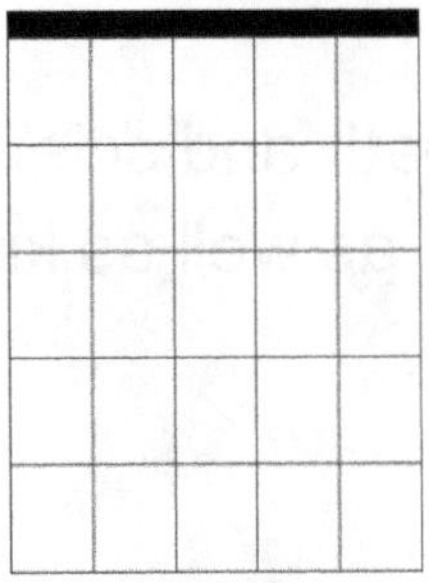 GM13 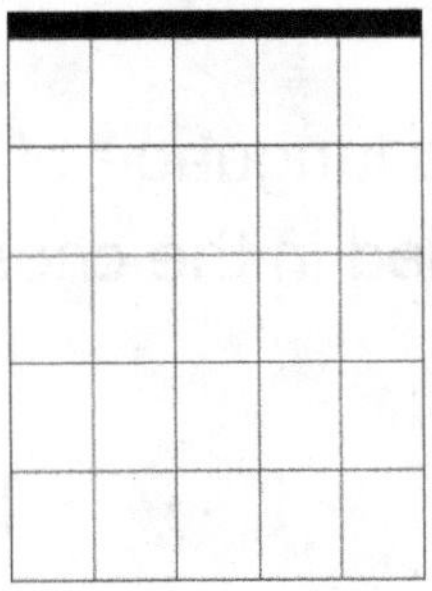 Am13

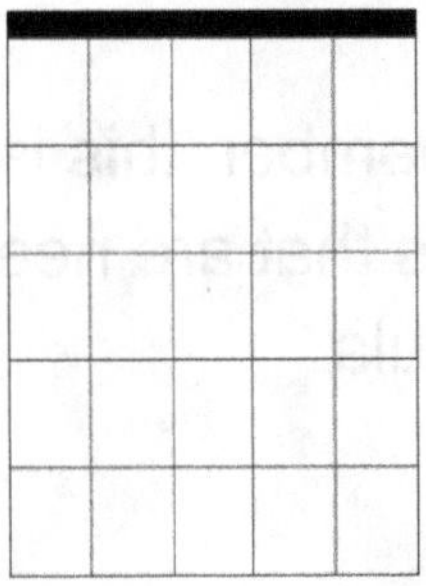

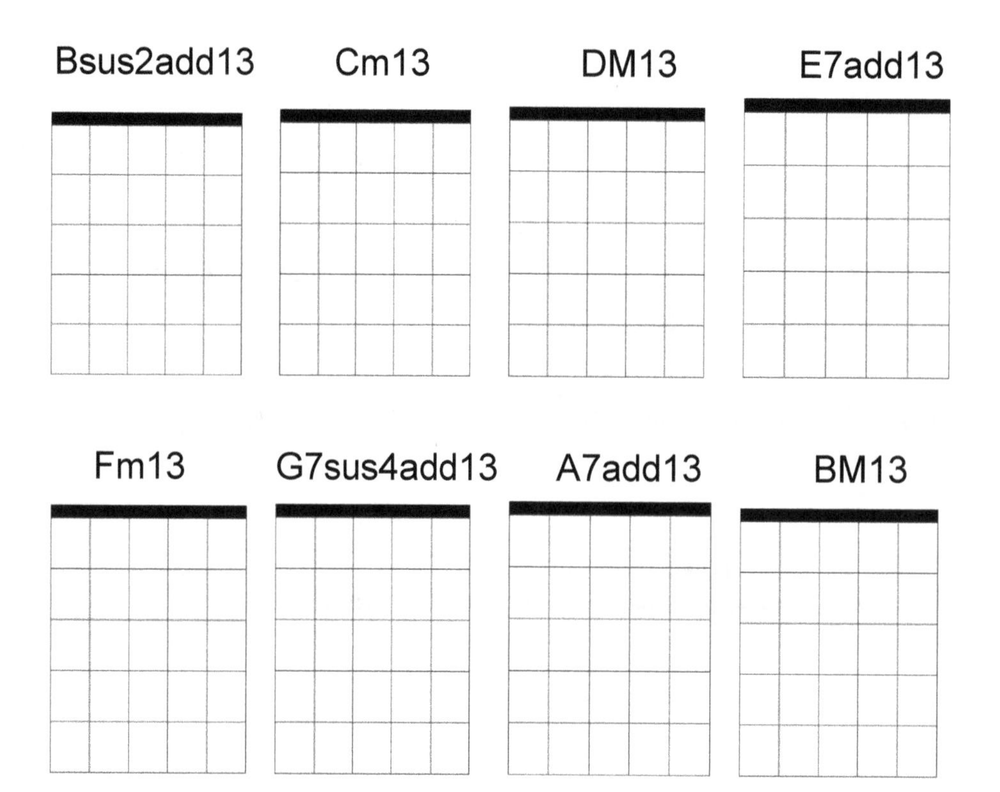

When going through these chord examples, make sure to write out as much as you can. The correct note location as well as the chord formula.

Remember, this is a language of math and science. Know the notes that are needed in the chord, as well as know the chord formula.

Chapter 6 Summary

In this chapter we have looked at ways to create a thirteenth chord. Similar to the eleventh chords in the previous chapter. We can make major 13, minor 13, dominant 13, and suspended 13 chords. Actually more than that, but lets keep it simple.

Just like we made the eleventh chords. Remember, the 13th chords are just a note added to the 7th chord. This allows us to create different shades of color.

First, we have the major 13th. A major 7th chord with a thirteenth added to it. 1 3 5 7 13

Second, we have the minor thirteenth chord. Once again, just a minor 7th with a thirteenth added to it. 1 b3 5 b7 13. Also be sure to remember that the minor seventh has two flats in it.

Third, we have the dominant thirteenth chord. Similar to the minor thirteenth except we keep the third note natural. This gives us a slightly different color. 1 3 5 b7 13.

Fourth, we have the suspended thirteenth chords. The 7sus2add13 as well as 7sus4add13. These allow us to create some additional colors. That is because the 13 is represented by the 6th note in the second octave.

Remember, these chords can have different names. They can be Major7add13, or m7add13, etc. This is common with the extended chords. Not too worry though, like I mentioned before they are different names for the same chord,

Fifth, I have presented you with thirteenth chord exercises. These are very important and should be filled out to make sure you know these chords.

You want to make sure you know how to create these chords on your guitar. And the more you study these chord charts, you'll get better at forming and writing these chords.

Chapter 7 Inversions & Extensions

Lesson 31: Chord inversions

A chord inversion is where the root of the chord (the 1) is not the lowest note. This means that another note in the chord occupies the bass position.

What this does is it allows us to create even more shades of color. And that is what learning chord theory is all about. Creating multiple shades of color. And this is done through chord inversions.

If you look at all the chords we've learned so far, you can clearly see that some of them have different notes in the bass. Sometimes it's the 1, sometimes it's the 5th, and with the extended chords, it's sometimes the 7th.

Let's take the C major chord for instance. The C major triad is made up of three notes, the C E and G. The root of the chord (the 1) is normally the lowest note.

But let's say you come across a C major chord where the G (the 5th) is the lowest note. This would be considered a C major chord inversion.

Basic chord types are built with the notes arranged in the order or root, third, and fifth. You can see this in the lessons on triads. But in order to expand these chords, we need to use inversions. Where we change the order of the notes.

They're still the same notes, just in a different order. Depending on what note is in the bass will determine what chord inversion it is.

If the 1 is in the lowest note, this is considered the root.

If the 3rd is the lowest note, this is considered 1st inversion.

If the 5th is the lowest note, this is considered 2nd inversion.

If the 6th or 7th is the lowest note, this is considered the 3rd inversion.

And if the 9th is the lowest note, this is considered the 4th inversion.

Go back and look at all the chords that you have learned so far in this book. You will see clearly which ones are inversions.

All chords come down to a scientific formula.

Major: 1 3 5
Minor: 1 b3 5
Sus2: 1 2 5
Sus4: 1 4 5
Major 6: 1 3 5 6
Minor 6: 1 b3 5 6
Major 7: 1 3 5 7
Minor 7: 1 b3 5 b7
Dom7: 1 3 5 b7
Dom 9: 1 3 5 b7 9
Major 9: 1 3 5 7 9
Minor 9: 1 b3 5 b7 9
Etc, etc, etc.

Chord inversions are what allow you to create thousands of chords on the guitar. Can you see how many more chords you could create from the above example by just moving some of the notes around within each chord?

The other way to create more chords is with chord extensions and alternates. Remember, once you go past 7, you proceed into the next octave or series of notes in the same order. This is what allows for all these different chords

Let's now look at chord extensions and alterations.

Lesson 32: Chord extensions

A chord extension is what we have already learned with some of our chords such as 9ths, 11ths, and 13ths. These are extensions of the basic triad. This alone allows us to create more chords. But we can create even more than that.

Let's look at the key of C major for instance:

C D E F G A B C
1 2 3 4 5 6 7 8

As we can see from the knowledge that we have gained so far, we can create multiple chords out of this key.

C Major: 1 3 5= C E G
C Major6: 1 3 5 6= C E G A
C Major7: 1 3 5 7= C E G B
Csus2: 1 2 5= C D G
Csus4: 1 4 5= C F G
Csus2add7: 1 2 5 7= C D G B
Csus4dd7: 1 4 5 7= C F G B
Etc, Etc, Etc.

Do you see how this works? These are what's called chord extensions. We can even create more chords with alternate notes like a #5 or b6.

We could create a Cm#5b7 chord. 1 3 #5 b7. Or a CM7b6 chord. 1 3 5 b6 7. Or even a C7#5b9 chord. 1 3 #5 b7 b9.

Do you see how we can create even more chords with this knowledge of notes and chord formulas?

By applying different inversions, extensions and alterations within any chord shape, you can create a multitude of chord variations. And if you can do this on all six strings, the sky's the limit on what you can create.

But in order to do so, you must fully understand how this knowledge works. And not just in theory. You want to be able to look at your guitar fretboard and know exactly where each note is located on each string.

Only then will you be able to fully apply what you've learned in this book. Remember, all knowledge of any subject has two phases to it. Theory and practical application. Make sure that when it comes to guitar playing, you master both.

Lesson 33: Six/nine chords

Six nine chords are another type of chord extension that can be played to create some nice shades of color. These can be played within every triad that has been learned so far. This is where we add the 6 and 9th notes together.

This creates a 6/9 chord. Or you could also call it a 6add9 chord. Once again, two different names for the same chord. Usually we don't add a 9 until we get past the 7. That is why I presented the chords the way I did in the previous lessons.

This makes them easier to build and learn. But like I said in the last two chapters, this gives us a way to create even more chords. So the 6/9 chord formula would be 1 3 5 6 9.

CM6: 1 3 5 6
C6/9: 1 3 5 6 9

We can do this with minor, augmented, and diminished chords.

Cm6: 1 b3 5
Cm6/9: 1 b3 5 6 9
Caug6/9: 1 3 #5 6 9
Cdim6/9: 1 b3 b5 6 9

See how this allows us to create even more chords?

When you start adding notes together and moving them around, there really is no limit to the kinds of chords you can create. Although they must have the fundamental foundation in them. So don't forget that.

You can't just put a random group of notes together and call it a chord. They must fit together in harmony with each other.

And as you work with the practical application side of it more (applying this knowledge to your fretboard) you'll begin to hear how notes vibrate in harmony with each other. And how others don't.

Six/nine chords are great because they give a different type of color that is a little bit off from the other chords presented.

Even if you don't use them much, I recommend you learn how to from them. The more you can put this information into practical use, the better you'll be at playing the guitar.

But like I said before, you must practice and work with it. Daily if at all possible. This will allow it to stick in your head more and be ready when you need it most.

Lesson 34: Chord Progressions

Once you know a few chords, you then want to start putting them together to create chord progressions. These are the foundation of any contemporary song. You first learn to form the chords, and then put them together to create music.

In this lesson I'm going to present you with a few progression examples that you can work with. Using some of the chords that you have learned. Do you happen to know how many that is? How many you've learned so far?

Let's look at some chord progression examples.

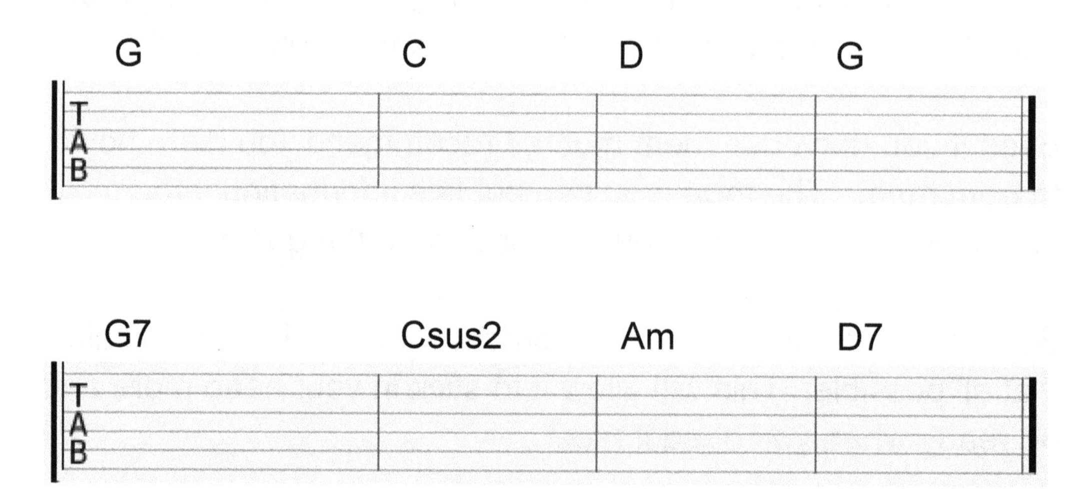

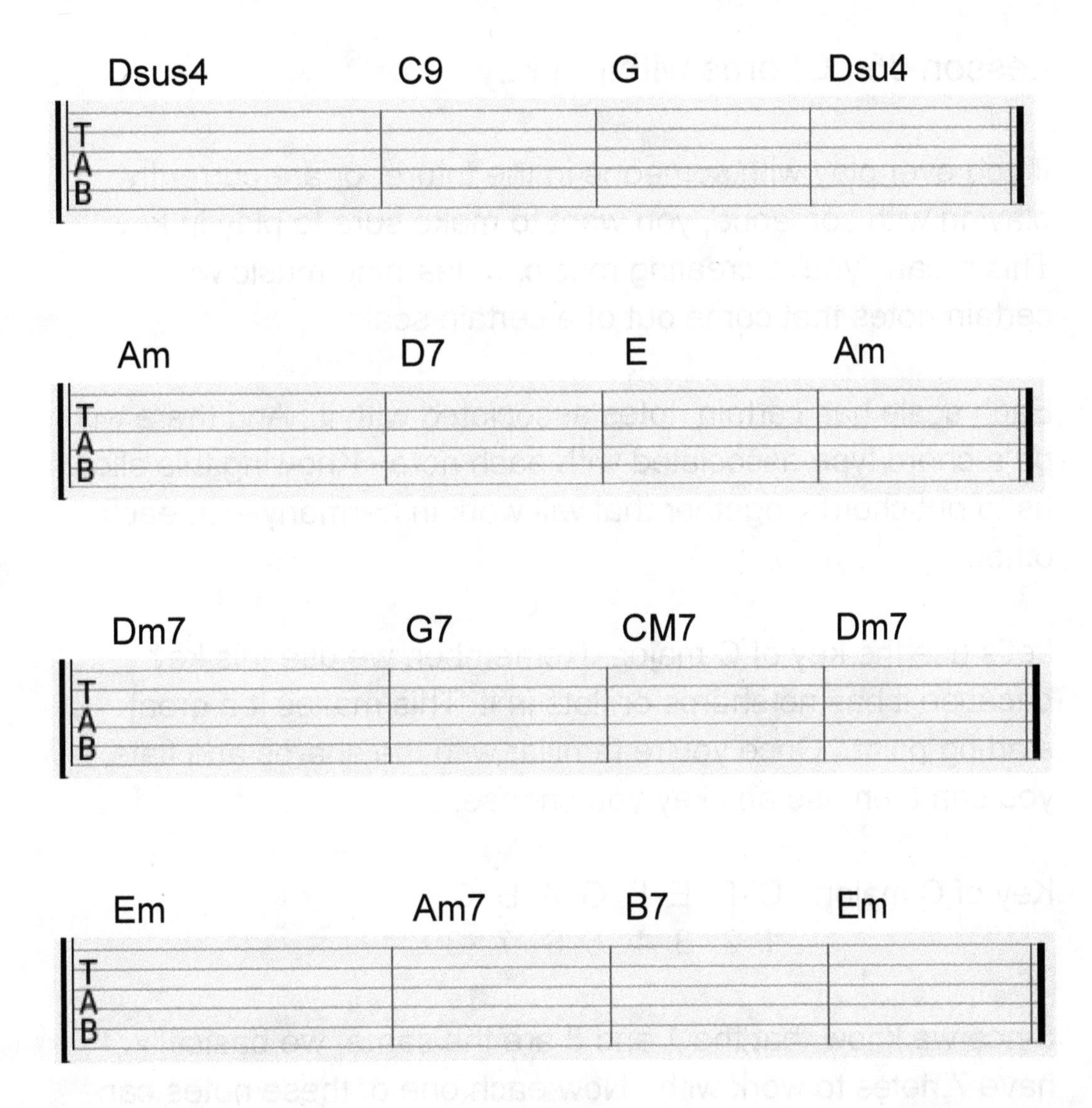

I kept these simple for easier learning, but see how they sound when you add chord extensions. Listen for how they change the shade of color. You'll eventually begin to hear these chords in some of your favorite songs.

Lesson 35: Chords within a key

If you ever play with someone in the future, or are currently playing with someone, you want to make sure to play in key. This means you're creating music, or learning music with certain notes that come out of a certain scale.

Each scale has certain notes associated with it. And there will be a chord type associated with each note. Knowing this allows us to put chords together that will work in harmony with each other.

Let's use the key of C major. Remember, we use this key because it has no sharps or flats in it. This makes it a great starting point. Once you're familiar with the sharps and flats, you can then use any key you choose.

Key of C major: C D E F G A B C
1 2 3 4 5 6 7 8

Since we know that the 1 and 8 are the same, we basically have 7 notes to work with. Now each one of these notes can relate to a certain type of chord. To remember this easier, we can break it down into a simple formula.

Let's now look at this simple formula for easier learning.

1 = major
2 = minor
3 = minor
4 = major
5 = major
6 = minor
7 = diminished

This goes for any major key you choose to work in. So for the key of C that I mentioned earlier, the chords would be;

1 C major
2 D minor
3 E minor
4 F major
5 G major
6 A minor
7 B diminished.

See if you can figure this out in all the other major keys. What would the chords be for A major, B major, D major, etc. This basic chord theory will help you out in song writing, learning songs, and staying in key when jamming with others.

Remember, music is a language. Give it time to develop.

Chapter 7 Summary

In the seventh chapter we have learned some great insights to how we can create multiple chords out of just one. This is through chord inversions. What note is in the lowest position, as well as creating chord extensions.

First, we learn about chord inversions. This is where certain notes like the 3rd, 5th, 7th, or 9th are in the bass. This allows us to create multiple shades of the same color. Very helpful when painting with guitar chords.

Remember the 3rd is first inversion, 5th is second, 6th, or 7th is third, and 9th is the fourth. Knowing this will allow you to expand your knowledge of guitar chords.

Second, we have chord extensions. Anything past the 7th note in the first octave is a chord extension. The 9, 11, and 13 are all chord extensions. Knowing this information allows us to be able to build chords past the first octave.

Inversions and extensions are what allow thousands, and I do mean thousands of chords to be created on the guitar. I know it seems weird huh? But it's true.

Third, we have six/nine chords. These are a bit off of the beaten path as they are kind of a hybrid. Using the 6th in the first octave and just adding the 9th from the second octave and leaving out the 7th.

Normally we use the 7th note in the chord when creating chord extensions, but in this case, to create this chord type we eliminate it.

Fourth, we learn about chord progressions. These are how we put chords together to create music. Chords by themselves don't really do anything. It's when you put them together that they start to really sound pleasant to the ear.

Go through the progressions presented in the lesson and listen for how they sound, then try substituting the chords for chord inversions and extensions. This will really help you get a solid grasp of chords and how to put them together.

Fifth, we learn about chords within a major key. Each of the 7 notes in a major key have certain chords that relate to it. There are three majors, three minors and one diminished. Knowing this and which ones they are will help you with song writing, learning songs, and staying in key when jamming.

Study this chapter well and practice the exercises presented. It will help you to develop a better understanding of music theory.

Chapter 8: Barre chords

Lesson 36: Root 6 barre chords

In this final chapter we are going to look at barre chords. These are what you use to play chords further up the fretboard. We touched on these already in some of the chords we've already learned, but we'll go more in-depth here.

All the chords we've learned so far (except for a couple) are all played in the open position. Around the first few frets. In this lesson we'll look at root 6 barre chords. As these and root 5 barre chords are the most commonly used.

A barre chord is where you place your index finger across the strings to create a barre. This is basically using your finger to represent the nut. What this does, is it allows you to move open chords further up the fretboard.

It also allows you to play in other keys that are represented further up the fretboard. Also what's great about barre chords, is that the shape of the chord stays the same. You just need to move it up or down the fretboard.

Let's look at a few examples.

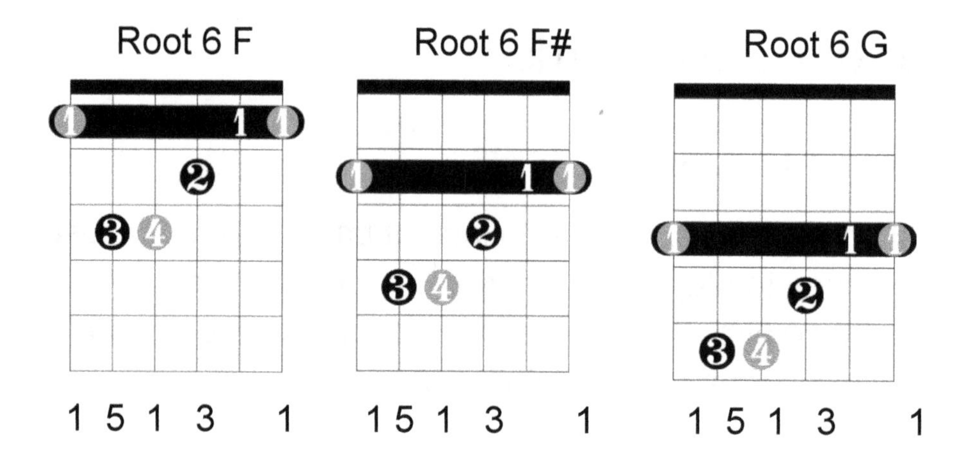

Can you see what I mean by them all having the same shape?

Can you see how they all have the major triad in them?

Can you see that if you remove the second finger, you would have a root 6 minor barre chord?

Can you see how the root of the chord is on the 6th string?

Can you see how you just move the shape up the fretboard to change the name of the chord?

They are all the same, it's just where they are located on the fretboard that makes them different. This is how you play chords further up the neck.

And if you know your notes, you just add them to the chord shape to create sus4, m7, add9, etc, etc, etc.

Lesson 37: Root 5 barre chords

These types of chords are the same thing. The only difference is that the root of the chord will be on the fifth string instead of the sixth. The root 6 work off of the E and E minor chords, as the root 5 work off of A and A minor.

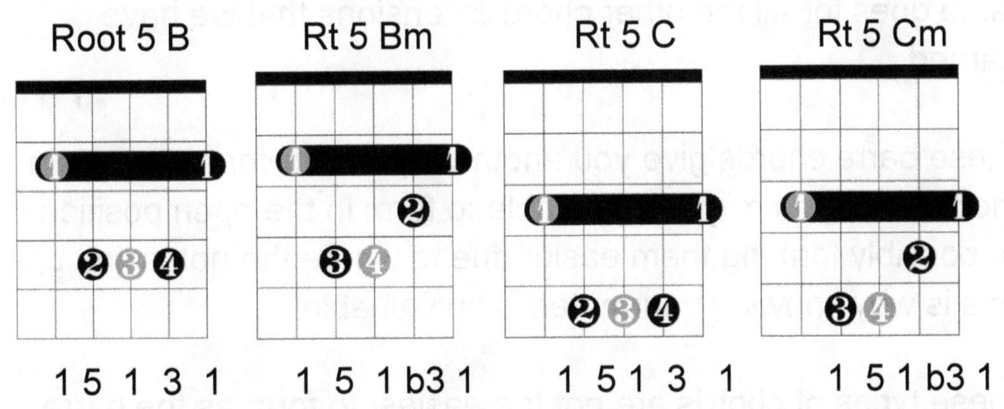

Can you see how these are the same thing as the root 6 barre chords, just on the 5th string?

Can you see how the A major triad is in the major chords, and the A minor triad is in the minor chords?

Can you see how we just move the 3rd note back one fret and it becomes a b3rd?

Can you see how the chords are the same shape, but change name because of their location on the fretboard?

As before, add other notes to create additional chords.

Like I mentioned before, these chord types are built off of the E and A triads. When you look at the chord chart, you can clearly see them in there. If you want to make an augmented barre chord, just add it in there.

The same goes for diminished, sus2, and sus4 triads. The same goes for all the other chord extensions that we have learned.

These barre chords give you another option for forming certain chords, that you might not be able to form in the open position. Or possibly forming them easier due to where the notes line up. This is why knowing your notes is so valuable.

These types of chords are not the easiest to form as the barre does require some strength in your index finger to hold down all the strings. But this will get better through practice.

Lesson 38: Single finger barre chords

These types of chords are what I would call a partial barre chord. As you will see when you learn songs, many guitar players play partial chords. Sometimes partial open chords, and sometimes partial barre chords.

These single finger barre chords will be based off of the A major triad. Can be formed with a single finger and moved up the fretboard.

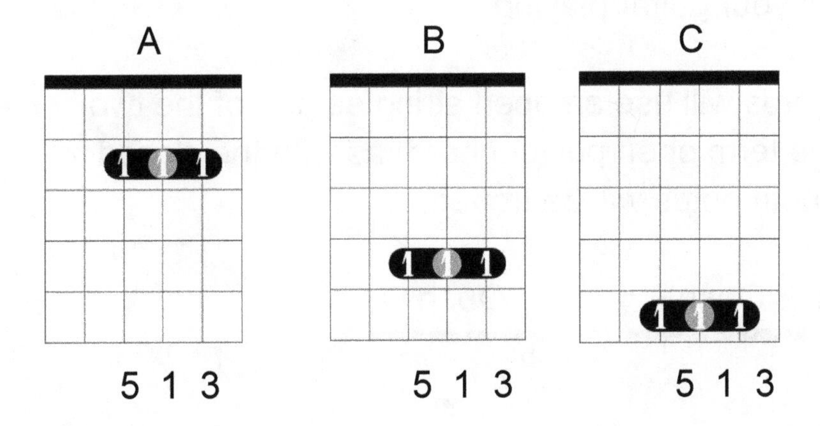

These are another chord shape you can make with the A major triad. And just like with the full barre chords, these shapes are exactly the same. You just move them up the fretboard to change chords.

These chord types are very popular and a good way for you to abbreviate traditional barre chords.

Lesson 39: Power chords

These are another very popular abbreviation of the full barre chord. The infamous power chord. It is named this because it is made up of only two notes and when you add distortion, it sounds very powerful.

These chord types are very popular in rock music where distortion is a huge part of the overall guitar tone. We have open power chords, and closed power chords. Both can be very essential in your guitar playing.

Open power chords will use an open string as one of the two notes (hence the term open power chord) as with the closed power chords, both notes will be fretted.

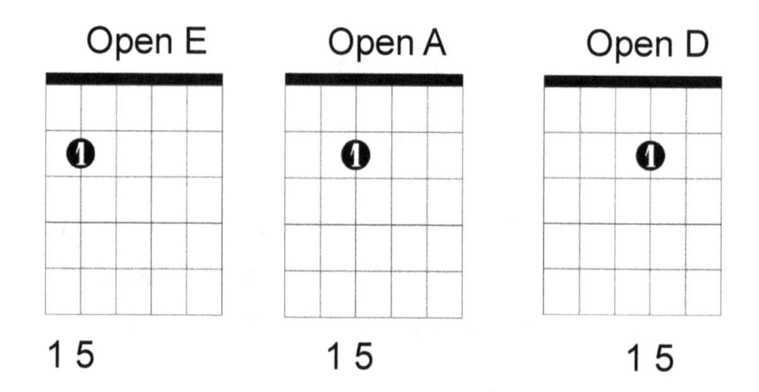

These are probably the easiest chords to play on the guitar. As you can see, they only require one finger.

Although, the chord we learned earlier that didn't have any fretted noted would be easier. But as far as power chords are concerned, these would be the easiest.

As you can see, we use the open string as the root note. That is why they are called open power chords. Because the root note is open.

They are also called 5 chords. This is because the two notes used in the chord are the 1 and 5. These types of chords eliminate the 3. So they are neither major or minor, but lean more towards the minor than the major.

Closed power chords work the same. Just the 1 and 5th notes are used. Sometimes you'll see the octave note thrown in as a third note. This makes the chord a bit fuller, but still made up of the 1 and 5.

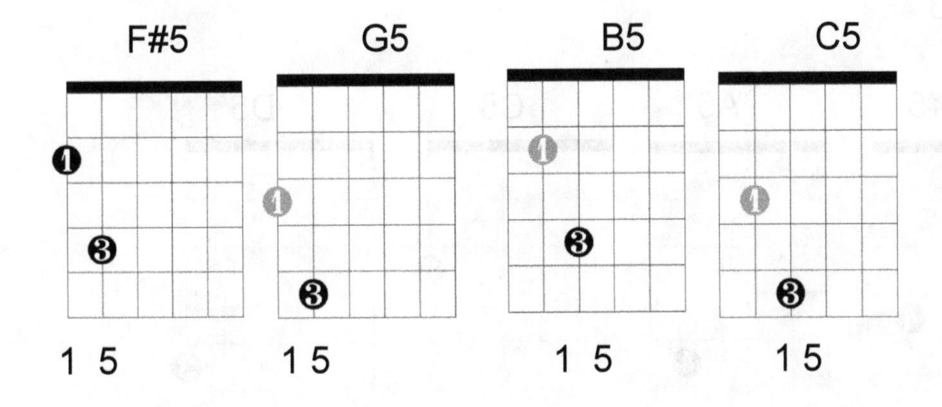

As you can see, these are all the same, just in different places.

These can also be formed and played on the fourth string. Same shape and same fingering.

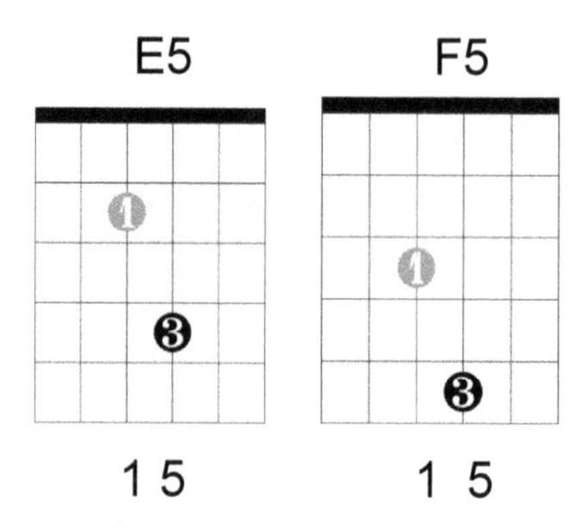

Remember, since the root note is on a particular string, that will be the name of the chord. Root 6, root 5, etc. You can also play root 3 and root 2 power chords.

The only thing with the root 3 is we'll need to move the 5th note up a fret because of the B string. The root 2 won't need to be adjusted.

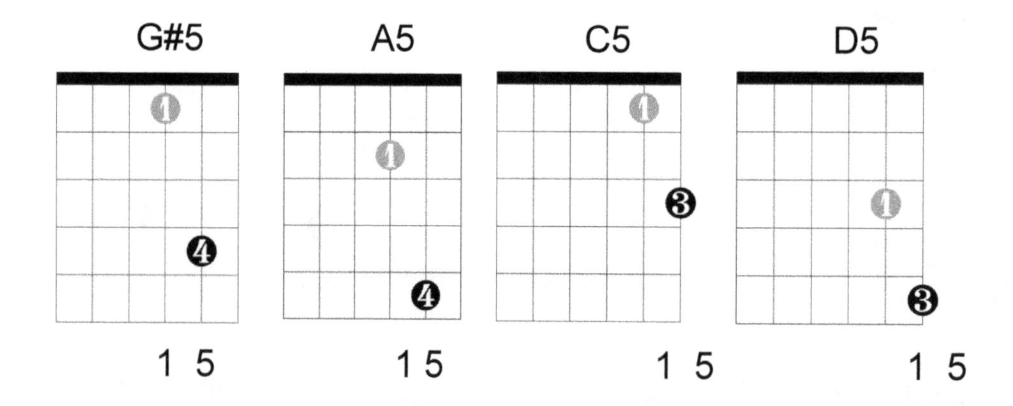

As you can see with these types of chords, you just move them around the fretboard to change the chord name.

Although the name changes because the notes change, the shape of the chord stays the same. That is the true benefit of these types of chords.

They do require a bit of a stretch at first, but all the other chords you learned in the previous lessons should have helped you develop this already. If not, just keep at it.

I recommend you use your index and ring finger to play these chords. That is the most common way, plus it keeps the fourth finger available for note extensions.

Although I have seen many guitar players play these chords with the first and fourth fingers. This will be very beneficial for the root 2 power chords where the note moves up a fret.

It doesn't really matter what fingers you choose to use, all that matters is that you get the chords down and understand how to form them. This last lesson will help with that.

Lesson 40: Power chord exercises

Once again I present you will chord exercises. This will allow you to make sure that you know and can play these chords very well. Remember, all these chords are how you play further up the fretboard.

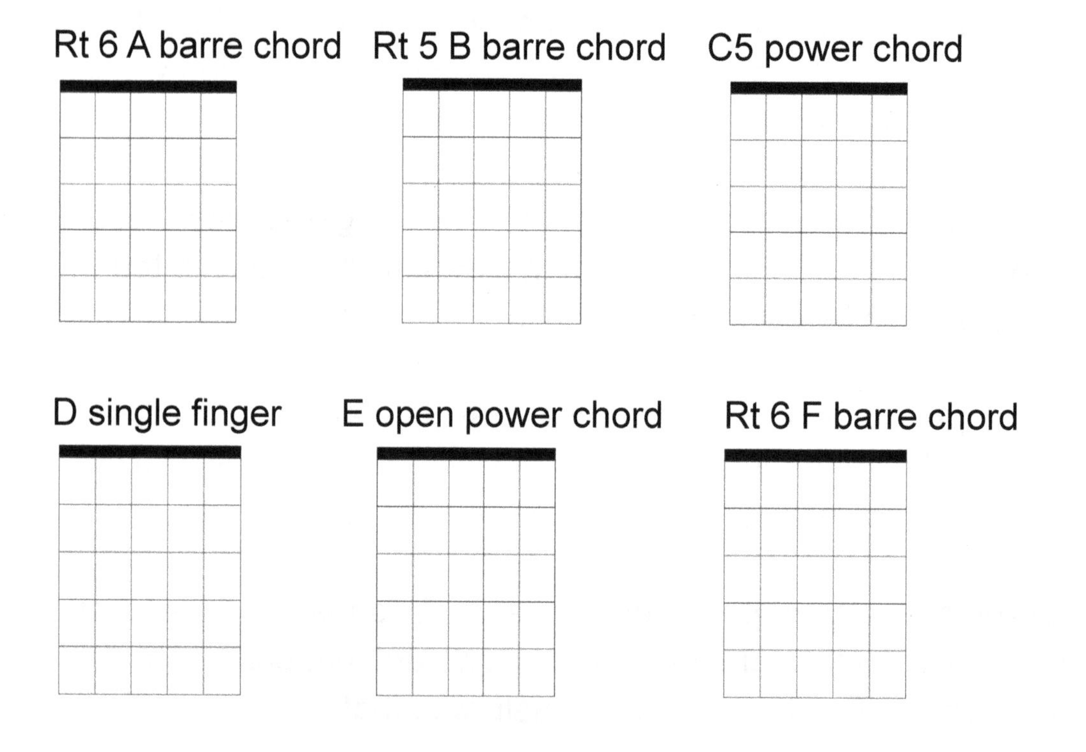

Remember that the single finger chords are based on moving the A major triad up and down the fretboard. A single finger type of partial barre chord.

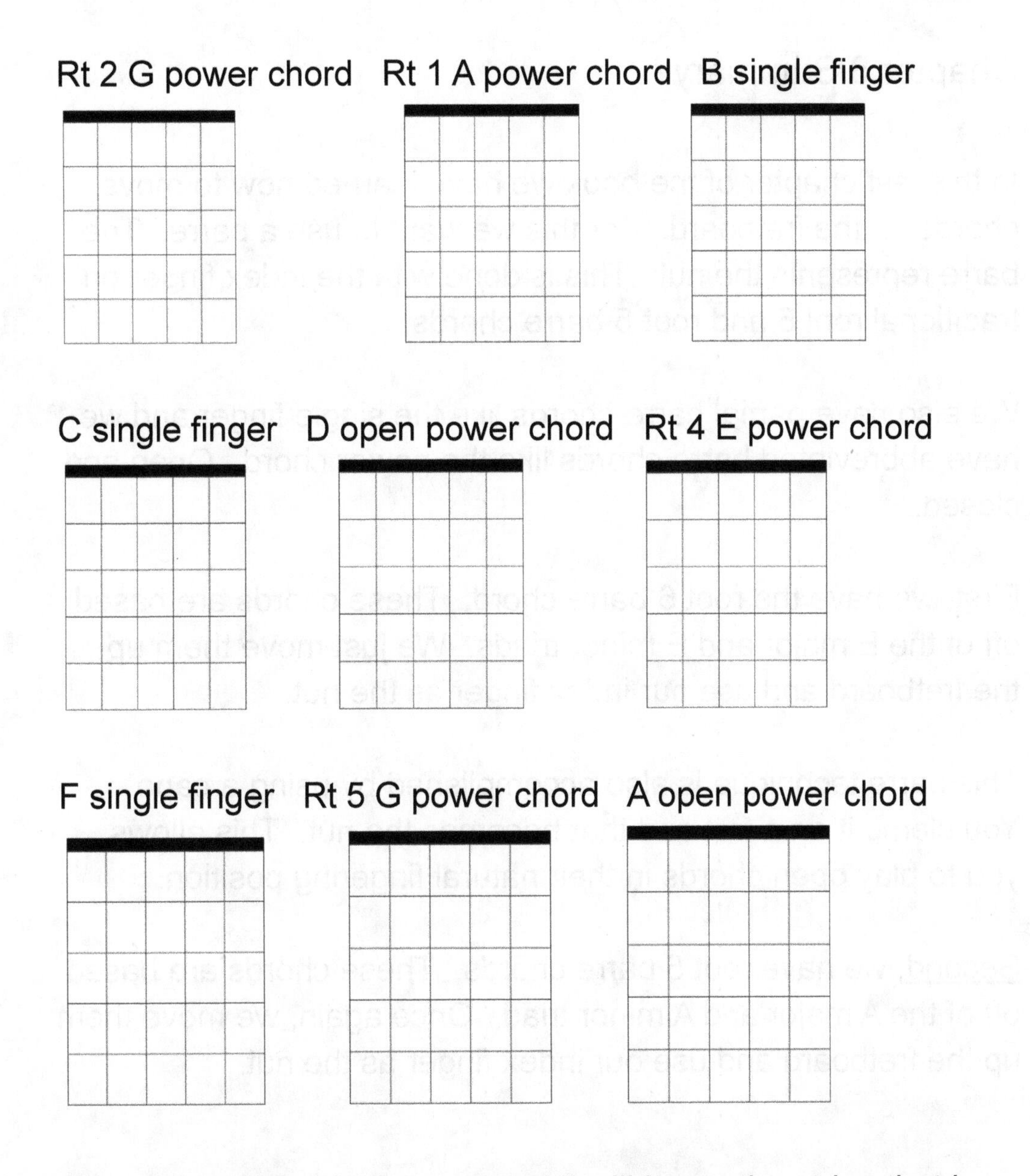

Remember, the 1 is the root and it will be on the string that is specified. Root 5 will be on the fifth string, root 6 and open will be on the sixth string. These are very popular chords in rock music, so make sure you know them very well.

Chapter 8 Summary

In this last chapter of the book we have learned how to move chords up the fretboard. For this we want to use a barre. The barre represents the nut. This is done with the index finger on traditional root 6 and root 5 barre chords.

We also have partial barre chords like the single finger and we have abbreviated barre chords like the power chord. Open and closed.

First, we have the root 6 barre chord. These chords are based off of the E major and E minor triads. We just move them up the fretboard and use our index finger as the nut.

This barre technique is also accomplished by using a capo. You clamp it on a fret and that becomes the nut. This allows you to play open chords in their natural fingering position.

Second, we have root 5 barre chords. These chords are based off of the A major and A minor triad. Once again, we move them up the fretboard and use our index finger as the nut.

Third, we have single finger barre chords. These are based off of the A major triad as well. These are a played with any single finger. They allow us to move chords quickly without having to form the whole barre. They create a different shade of color.

Fourth, we have the infamous power chords. These are also called 5 chords. A5, D5, G5, etc. A simple two note chord that is an abbreviated barre chord. Sometimes three notes are used if you add the octave.

We have open power chords that use the open strings as the root, and we have closed power chords where both notes are fretted.

Fifth, we have barre chord exercises. I highly recommend you go through these, write them out here in the book. Make sure you know how to form them and where they are located on the fretboard.

As I said before, these types of chords are very popular in rock music and work extremely well with music that has distortion on the guitar.

Chord Formula Quiz

Now I present you with a way to gauge how well you've done with the training. This is a simple test for you and you alone. A chance to see what lessons have been learned and what lessons still need to be worked on.

Music is a language, and like all other languages can seem a bit foreign at first. Especially with its unfamiliar concepts. In this case, chord formulas. The better you know these chord formulas, the quicker you'll be able to find and play them.

Each question is from a lesson. So if you don't know something or can't remember, just go back and review the lesson the question came out of.

Q: What formula makes up any major triad?
A: ______________________________

Q: What formula makes up any minor triad?
A: ______________________________

Q: What formula makes up any augmented triad?
A: ______________________________

Q: What formula makes up any diminished triad?
A: ______________________________

Q: What formula makes up any sus2 triad?
A: ______________________________

Q: What formula makes up any sus4 triad?
A: ______________________________

Q: What formula makes up any major six chord?
A: ______________________________

Q: What formula makes up any minor six chord ?
A: ______________________________

Q: What formula makes up a sus2 six chord?
A: ______________________________

Q: What formula makes up a sus4 six chord?
A: ______________________________

Q: What formula makes up a major seventh chord?
A: ______________________________

Q: What formula makes up a minor seventh chord?
A: ______________________________

Q: What formula makes up any dominant seventh chord?
A: ____

Q: What formula makes up any suspended seventh chord?
A: ____

Q: What formula makes up any major ninth chord ?
A: ____

Q: What formula makes up any minor ninth chord?
A: ____

Q: What formula makes up any dominant ninth chord?
A: ____

Q: What formula makes up any suspended ninth chord?
A: ____

Q; What formula makes up any major eleventh chord?
A: ____

Q; what formula makes up any minor eleventh chord?
A: ____

Q: What formula makes up any dominant eleventh chord?
A: ____

Q: What formula makes up any suspended eleventh chord?
A: ____

Q: What formula makes up any major thirteenth chord?
A: ____

Q: What formula makes up any minor thirteenth chord?
A: ____

Q: What formula makes up any dominant thirteenth chord?
A: ____

Q: What formula makes up any suspended thirteenth chord?
A: ____

Q: What is a chord inversion?
A: ____

Q: What is a chord extension?
A: ____

Q: What is a six/nine chord?
A: ____

Q: What are chord progressions?
A: ____

Q: What chords are in every major key?
A: ____

Q: What chords make up the root 6 barre chords?
A: ____

Q: What chords make up the root 5 barre chords?
A: ____

Q: What chord makes up the single finger barre chords?
A: ____

Q: What is a power chord?
A: ____

Q: What two notes make up the power chord?
A: ____

Q: Why is it called a power chord?
A: ____

Q: What are open power chords?
A: ____

Q: How many open power chords are presented?
A: ____

Q: What is different about the root 2 power chord?
A: ____

Q: How many chords have you learned in this book?
A; ____

** If you need to make additional notes, feel free to write here on this page. It is left blank for this purpose**

Learn Guitar Chord Theory Conclusion

In this training manual we have learned a lot about how chords are constructed and how to embellish them to create new chords. This will give you more insight into how the notes on the guitar work in harmony with each other.

This will also give you insight to scales. Because chords and scales as they are both made up of the same building blocks. Scales work very much in the same way. A major scale will have a natural third, and a minor scale a flat third.

By starting out with triads and building from there, you'll begin to build a solid foundation of how music in general (no matter the instrument played) works. This will help you with learning and writing songs.

In addition to that you get better acquainted with your guitar fretboard. When you create guitar chords and think about the notes, it stimulates your brain waves. It also develops inner sight to see the notes better to easily form the chords.

You start to develop a better understanding of how to produce emotion with your guitar. Like an artist who paints with different shades of color. So you too will be able to express yourself in the same way with guitar chords.

These are not all the chords that you can form. Nearly just a foundation to build upon. With so many chords that can be created, this book would be the size of an encyclopedia. No need for that, just a reference guide of the ones most common.

Remember, there's a learning curve. This is always present with new information. Practice patience and discipline. Give yourself time to digest the material and your fingers time to adjust to the fretboard. Do this and you will be successful.

And if you need additional help with any of the lessons I teach in this book, feel free to shoot me an email through my website at_dwaynesguitarlessons.com. Or if you have success, reach out and let me know as I'd love to hear about it.

You can also contact me through any social media avenue as I am on just about everyone of them. It never hurts to reach out for help. That is what I'm here for. We can do an online lesson if need be.

Also be sure to check out my other books that I have authored as they will make a great addition to your guitar education.

Best of luck, and have fun.

Sincerely, Dwayne Jenkins

Other Books By Dwayne's Guitar Lessons

How To Play Electric Guitar

A beginners step-by-step guide to playing electric guitar.

How To Play Electric Guitar will teach you:

1. What guitar to choose
2. What type of amplifier is best
3. Chords best used for rhythm
4. Scales best used for solos

And many many, more things to help you develop the skill of playing electric guitar.

Learn To Play Acoustic Guitar

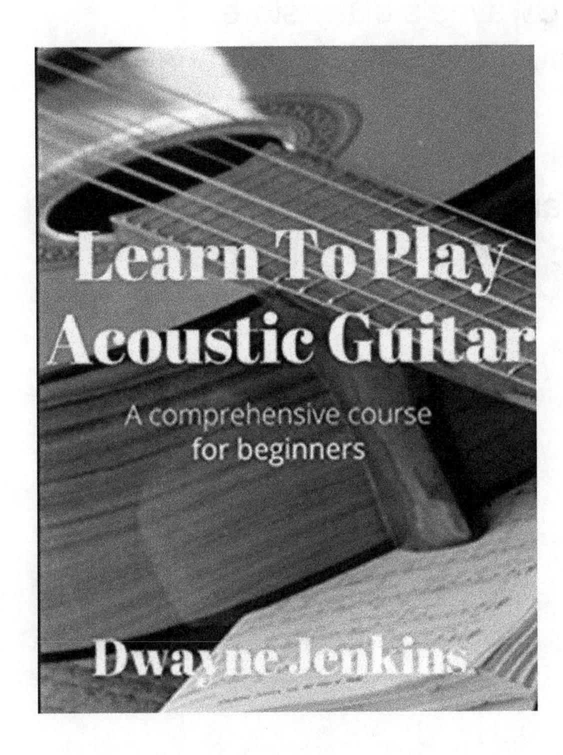

A simple step-by-step study on playing acoustic guitar.

Learn To Play Acoustic Guitar will teach you:

1. What kind of acoustic guitar to purchase
2. How to hold it for best playing results
3. Getting started with your first chords
4. How to read basic sheet music

And many more things that will get you playing the acoustic guitar in no time. A great addition to this book.

These and all other books authored by Dwayne can be purchased through Amazon or Dwayne's eBay store. If purchased at his eBay store, you will receive a "personally signed to you" author copy.

So be sure to check out all guitar books and lessons by Dwayne Jenkins. You'll be able to take your guitar playing to the next level.

Dwayne's Guitar World:

Along with teaching private guitar lessons throughout Denver Colorado and providing training guides, blog posts & videos, Dwayne also has an eBay store to provide you with additional inspiration.

Here you will find guitar strings, picks, straps, cleaners, rock & roll collectibles, and many other items to help you keep your guitar maintained and your skills at peak performance.

And of course the store would not be complete without his very own line of personally branded rock & roll apparel. Such things as t-shirts, baseball hats, beanies & coffee mugs. Which are all designed to provide you with inspiration to keep having fun.

So if you're looking for help in fueling your desire to learn guitar, look no further than Dwayne's Guitar World.

About the Author

Dwayne Jenkins is a self accomplished musician and a professional guitar teacher. He has been learning, playing and teaching guitar lessons throughout Denver, CO for almost two decades.

He is now bringing his special training skills and methodology that has been honed and hand-crafted throughout the years on how to play guitar to students around the world.

Dwayne has a unique exciting approach that gets students of all ages and skill levels enjoying the fun of playing guitar. His enthusiasm and love for teaching shine through with every lesson that he creates.

His lessons are designed to enhance your ability to progress. No matter your reason for learning guitar, there will always be something in Dwayne's guitar books and products to help you achieve your dreams.

So if you're a student looking to start, or a student looking to further your education, be sure to get involved with Dwayne's guitar lessons and learn what so many people have already discovered why learning to play guitar is one of the greatest things you can do for yourself.

What Students Are Saying About Dwayne's Guitar Books & Lessons

"The beginners instruction book Learn To Play Guitar Solos by Dwayne Jenkins is an excellent guide for playing lead guitar. It covers everything from scales, to learning to solo. Including ear training and harmonizing. The exercises are fun and make you want to learn more." **Cheryl**

"You really enjoy teaching and you know the fretboard like the back of your hand.I definitely recommend your books, and watching your videos. As always, great job Dwayne."
Mike

"Dwayne, thank you so much for everything you have taught me and done for me. You are an amazing guitarist and wonderful teacher" **BJ**

"Dwayne, thank you for being a great teacher and teaching me many great songs. This is a skill that will last me a lifetime."
Danielle

"I bought your How To Play Guitar Solos book, absolutely phenomenal so far. Was in a rut with my playing recently as I could play decent rhythm but struggled with soloing. Good Job man." **Euan**

“The book Learn To Play Acoustic Guitar is a sure path to learning how to play an acoustic guitar! It will provide a pleasant learning experience as it covers everything a beginner needs to know. The book is straightforward and it is really nice to be able to practice as you read through the lessons, not just read. There are plenty of examples and diagrams to help the reader understand how to play. I also really appreciated that you’re given recommendations on what type/brand of equipment is worth looking into for things like guitar picks or a tuner. Lastly I’d like to acknowledge that you’re also provided access for personal help, after all, nothing beats an actual teacher! All in all, This is an excellent book to get you started on playing acoustic guitar.” **Michelle**

“Dwayne, we want you to know we are honored to have you at the studio. We appreciate all that you do and are grateful that we can leave you in charge” **Angie & Wilson M.E.C**

“Dwayne, we are so glad you are our Teacher. It’s been three years already, can you believe it? Thank you again. You’re the best!” **Chelsey & Lucas**

“Dwayne’s book on How To Play Guitar Modes is a great guide on playing modes. It is well written and easily understandable. Designed in such a way that it doesn’t shoot over your head. Great job!” **Marc**

"Dwayne, thank you so much for being not only an awesome guitar teacher, but an awesome friend as well." **Kayla**

"Dwayne, thank you so much for all the years of doing lessons. You have been very patient with my progress and helped me to build confidence in myself and inspired me to follow my dreams. And in doing so you have become a great friend." **Jake**

"Dwayne, Thank you so much for teaching me every Saturday and not only teaching me guitar but also about life and helping me with setting my goals. You are a great teacher, mentor and the best friend ever." **Carson**

"There is not another person I would want to be teaching me guitar! His 1 on 1 teaching makes learning guitar very personal & exhilarating. He teaches at your pace and takes pride in what YOU want to learn. The best part...if Dwayne doesn't know a song a student wants to play, he takes time out the week to learn it. His teaching comes to life in my performance and has progressed over the last 8 years. Words cannot describe how amazing a teacher, rockstar and true friend Dwayne has become to me." **Dominic**

"Dwayne's books are well written and easy to follow. I would definitely recommend his books to anyone wanting to learn guitar. You can easily find them on Amazon." **Betty**

Printed in the USA
CPSIA information can be obtained
at www.ICGtesting.com
LVHW081739021023
759920LV00022B/661

9 781736 639306